Treating Child-Abusive Families

Intervention Based on Skills-Training Principles

APPLIED CLINICAL PSYCHOLOGY

Series Editors: Alan S. Bellack, *Medical College of Pennsylvania at EPPI, Philadelphia, Pennsylvania,* and Michel Hersen, *University of Pittsburgh, Pittsburgh, Pennsylvania*

FUTURE PERSPECTIVES IN BEHAVIOR THERAPY
Edited by Larry Michelson, Michel Hersen, and Samuel M. Turner

CLINICAL BEHAVIOR THERAPY WITH CHILDREN
Thomas Ollendick and Jerome A. Cerny

OVERCOMING DEFICITS OF AGING: A Behavioral Approach
Roger L. Patterson

TREATMENT ISSUES AND INNOVATIONS IN MENTAL RETARDATION
Edited by Johnny L. Matson and Frank Andrasik

REHABILITATION OF THE BRAIN-DAMAGED ADULT
Gerald Goldstein and Leslie Ruthven

SOCIAL SKILLS ASSESSMENT AND TRAINING WITH CHILDREN
An Empirically Based Handbook
Larry Michelson, Don P. Sugai, Randy P. Wood, and Alan E. Kazdin

BEHAVIORAL ASSESSMENT AND REHABILITATION OF THE TRAUMATICALLY BRAIN DAMAGED
Edited by Barry A. Edelstein and Eugene T. Couture

COGNITIVE BEHAVIOR THERAPY WITH CHILDREN
Edited by Andrew W. Meyers and W. Edward Craighead

TREATING CHILD-ABUSIVE FAMILIES
Intervention Based on Skills-Training Principles
Jeffrey A. Kelly

In preparation

ISSUES IN PSYCHOTHERAPY RESEARCH
Edited by Michel Hersen, Larry Michelson, and Alan S. Bellack

---

A Continuation Order Plan is available for this series. A continuation order will bring delivery of each new volume immediately upon publication. Volumes are billed only upon actual shipment. For further information please contact the publisher.

Treating Child-Abusive Families

Intervention Based on Skills-Training Principles

Jeffrey A. Kelly

University of Mississippi Medical Center
Jackson, Mississippi

Plenum Press • New York and London

Library of Congress Cataloging in Publication Data

Kelly, Jeffrey A.
Treating child-abusive families.

(Applied clinical psychology)
Bibliography: p.
Includes index.
1. Child abuse—Treatment. 2. Social learning. I. Title. II. Series.
RC569.5.C55K44 1983 616.85′82 83-17667
ISBN 0-306-41417-1

A Division of Plenum Publishing Corporation
233 Spring Street, New York, N.Y. 10013

Printed in the United States of America

Preface

During the past ten years, the problem of child abuse has been the subject of increased attention both in the professional community and among the general public. The reasons for this widespread recognition are clear. First, professionals of many disciplines deal with child-abusive families and do so in a variety of ways: Physicians, hospital staff, and teachers are often the first to assess a child as the victim of abuse; social workers and child-protective personnel investigate cases of suspected abuse; court and legal authorities make determinations concerning the needs of an abused child; and mental health professionals, including psychologists, social workers, and family counselors, often have responsibility for treating abusive families. Few clinical problems have received this kind of widespread interdisciplinary recognition and, given the nature and seriousness of child-abusive behavior, few problems receive such intensive attention within each profession's literature.

A second factor responsible for increased study of child abuse is the fact that violence directed toward children is probably the most extreme form of family dysfunction seen by counselors, therapists, and other practitioners. While other types of child-management and anger-control problems occur far more frequently, the consequences of child-abusive behavior are much more serious than the consequences of other problems seen in child or family clinics. It has been estimated that as many as 550,000 children are the targets of parental abuse in the country each year (Helfer & Kemper, 1976). Among those children brought to hospitals and determined to be the victims of physical abuse from their parents, mortality rates of 10% or higher have been reported (McRae, Ferguson, & Lederman, 1973; Smith & Hanson, 1974), while other studies project that up to 5000 children die each year as a result of nonaccidental injury caused by their parents (Helfer, 1973). Numerous investigators have described not only the long-term physical injuries sustained by some abused children (such as irreversible neurological impairment), but also the permanent psychological harm caused by physical violence from one's parents. For all of these reasons, child abuse is correctly viewed by practitioners as one of the most serious problems seen in families.

A third factor responsible for increased recent attention to child abuse is that both professionals and the general public have had great difficulty understanding why child abuse occurs and, as a result, have had equal difficulty developing empirically based treatment approaches for abusive families. Although a problem like child abuse is considered important and demanding of our attention, it is not yet well conceptualized, and a great deal of clinical and research "searching" for causes and treatments is likely to occur. In this regard, it is interesting to note that of the hundreds of studies conducted on child abuse, the vast majority appear primarily to *describe* some aspect of abusive behavior. Numerous reports have attempted to identify parent personality characteristics related to abusive behavior, to describe child characteristics that relate to increased susceptibility for abuse, to assist physicians in diagnosing cases of nonaccidental injury, and to delineate the incidence of child abuse in this country. Much more rare in the literature are efforts to integrate this descriptive knowledge base into conceptual models that carry direct, practical implications for the treatment of child-abusive families.

The purpose of this book is to assist mental health practitioners who, in their professional roles, are called upon to treat child-abusive families. The first two chapters summarize present knowledge concerning the scope and prevalence of physically child-abusive behavior and review some of the major characteristics of abusive parents and their children. In Chapter 3, this information is integrated into a social learning conceptual model that can both account for the development of child-abusive behavior patterns and also suggest appropriate methods of clinical information with these families. Thus, beyond simply reviewing "facts" concerning abuse, the chapter develops a conceptual/theoretical model with direct treatment implications.

The balance of the book is oriented specifically toward practitioners, counselors, and therapists. Chapter 4 presents a detailed description of clinical assessment techniques (including interview procedures, techniques for the assessment of parent–child interaction problems, parent self-monitoring procedures, and other measures) that can be used to develop an intervention plan for abusive parents. Chapters 5–8 outline the types of intervention that are often necessary to treat child-abusive families, such as training parents to use effective, reinforcement-based child-management skills rather than punitive, violent child control strategies (Chapters 5 and 6), teaching abusive parents anger-control skills (Chapter 7), and intervening to reduce other more general life-style risk factors that involve problems in joblessness, problem-solving ability, marital discord, and social isolation (Chapter 8). In each of these chapters, clinical research on the treatment approach is reviewed, especially as it relates to child-abusive families or other families with severe interaction problems. The chapters are intended to provide the practitioner with specific, practical suggestions and guidelines for using these techniques with families.

Consistent with the social-learning theory conceptual framework taken in this book, most of the treatment approaches described here rely on a skills-training behavior change model for parents. In some cases, the required skills training focuses specifically on changing an abusive parent's disciplinary style toward his or her child; child-management training that teaches parents to use reinforcement-based strategies rather than physical punishment to control a youngster's misbehavior is an example of this kind of skills training. In other cases, more complex intervention is needed; some parents also require treatment that helps them learn to solve everyday problems and control temper, thereby reducing general frustration and anger/arousal levels. Regardless of the exact nature of treatment called for in a particular case, the interventions described in this book are all intended to increase the child-abusive parent's repertoire of appropriate coping skills and to reduce the likelihood of continued family violence.

Treating Child-Abusive Families is intended primarily for professionals who see these families in ongoing treatment. For this reason, topics such as determining whether a child is an abuse victim based on the youngster's injuries, legal and judicial questions related to child abuse, and similar issues are not stressed in this book. However, because mental health professionals treating abusive families almost invariably have contact with other workers (such as caseworkers who first investigate abuse reports, court judges, physicians, and community resource support groups), the matter of interdisciplinary team coordination in a family's treatment is of importance. Chapter 9 discusses some of the practical issues that are encountered when the therapist or counselor consults with a family's welfare department caseworker, court judge, and others. While treating abusive families is of immediate concern to psychologists, social workers, and other counselors, efforts that can prevent or reduce the incidence of child abuse are equally important. Based on a social-learning conceptualization of why abuse occurs, it is possible to draw inferences not only for treatment but also for prevention. This is the subject of the book's final chapter.

A good deal of progress is now being made in the treatment of abusive families, and well-controlled treatment studies are appearing regularly in the literature. Whenever possible, the techniques described here are based directly on empirical findings with child-abusive families. However, certain treatment methods that seem highly relevant and important for abusive parents (such as anger-control training) have not yet been studied extensively with this specific population. Nonetheless, these techniques are included here because they appear to be clinically useful and because consideration of them may serve to stimulate further applied research on their effectiveness with child-abusive families.

Acknowledgments

A number of persons contributed to this book in both direct and indirect ways. One of the most important and direct contributors was David Wolfe, whose expertise and interest were responsible for the development of a child abuse treatment program within the Child Psychology Clinic at the University of Mississippi Medical Center. I deeply appreciate his collaboration and respect his already substantial contributions to the child abuse treatment field.

Karen Christoff and Doreen Fairbank devoted a great deal of their time and talents to researching subjects for this book and provided many helpful suggestions during its development. Wauline Carter's assistance in preparing the manuscript was superb. My faculty colleagues and the psychology residents at the Medical Center have provided a stimulating clinical and research setting conducive to work in this area, and Michel Hersen was encouraging of my efforts to write this book. Finally, a special thanks must go to Krystal Numbers 4 and 5, where most of this book was written.

Contents

1

The Incidence and Scope of Child-Abusive Behavior

Maltreatment of children by their parents is not a new development in the history of societies. As investigators like Burgess (1979) and Steele (1976) have pointed out, violence within families has probably existed since the early beginnings of civilization when family units first developed. In ancient Rome, children were considered the property of their parents; fathers could, if they so desired, kill their own offspring with complete legal impunity. In Biblical times, there are frequent accounts of children being sacrificed or killed, such as when the Pharaoh directed the killing of all Hebrew children (Exodus 1:15, 1:22) and when King Herod ordered that all male children under two years of age be murdered (Matthew 2:16).

Severe disciplinary practices, of the type that would today be considered abusive, continued to be practiced through later centuries, usually embedded in the context of prevailing harsh attitudes concerning the submissive, propertylike role of children and the utility of punishment to overcome "wickedness." For example, Massachusetts in the early 1600s adopted a "Stubborn Child Act" which prescribed that rebellious or stubborn children past the age of understanding and nonobedient toward their parents could be put to death (see Fraser, 1976). As Steele (1976) notes, some abusive parents seek (and find) justification for their actions even in Biblical passages: "Withhold not correction from the child: for if thou beatest him with the rod, he shall not die. Thou shalt beat him with the rod, and shalt deliver his soul from hell" (Proverbs 23:13–14).

Abusive behavior toward children is certainly not limited to societies within the Judeo-Christian heritage. Anthropological studies of many cultures, both primitive and advanced, reveal that instances of extreme parental punitiveness can be found almost universally (Korbin, 1977). Abusive discipline of children, then, is neither a new phenomenon nor a pattern associated with any single cultural heritage.

While excessively harsh treatment of children by their parents is not a recent development, the recognition that it is a serious problem requiring intervention came much later. One of the earliest reported legal interventions on behalf of an abused child occurred in 1874, when authorities in New York found a girl beaten and tied to her bed. Because there were no applicable child abuse statutes at that time, intervention was made in the case of the American Society for the Prevention of Cruelty to Animals (Blumberg, 1974). A Society for the Prevention of Cruelty to *Children* was not founded until slightly later.

Fortunately, progress in the handling of child abuse cases has developed much more rapidly over the past twenty years. All states now have relatively uniform procedures requiring that cases of suspected child maltreatment be reported and all states now provide legal protection for those individuals who do report cases of suspected abuse. Children themselves are covered under two types of statutes, those which provide a range of child welfare protective services (to ensure the safety and well-being of the child) and those under which parents can be criminally charged in cases of serious abuse.

We will discuss the sociolegal aspects of child abuse investigation in more detail later in this chapter. However, let us first turn our attention to defining child-abusive behavior and considering its incidence and scope.

1.1. WHAT IS CHILD ABUSE?

The first major clinical definition of child abuse is usually credited to Kempe who, in 1962, outlined what he termed "the battered child syndrome." According to Kempe and his colleagues (Kempe, Silverman, Steele, Droegenmueller, & Silver, 1962) the major feature of this syndrome is the presence of an intentionally inflicted physical injury to the child, often a bone fracture, subdural hematoma, and/or multiple soft tissue injuries. The initial Kempe *et al.* (1962) report further suggested that (1) mortality and permanent brain injury occur in a relatively large number of abuse cases; (2) children who are most likely to be battered are under three years old; (3) signs of poor hygiene, malnutrition, and neglect may also be observed in these children; and (4) battering parents show "character defects" and aggression control problems, but are not always identifiable as sociopathic or psychotic.

One of the major effects of the early work by Kempe *et al.* (1962), as well as that by Fontana (1964), who outlined a similar syndrome, was alerting physicians to the fact that certain injuries to children are nonaccidental and that an inflicted injury pattern can be clinically assessed. This, in turn, led to further descriptive research on the types of injuries sustained by abused children and to conceptual distinctions among physical child abuse, sexual abuse, and neglect.

1.1.1. Physical Injuries Caused by Parental Abuse

Following early articles which described the need for physicians to recognize injuries inflicted on children by their parents (Fontana, 1964; Kempe *et al.*, 1962), a number of investigators conducted surveys to determine the types of injuries most often associated with abuse. In general, these reports are based on the physical injuries of children seen in hospital emergency rooms and pediatric departments. According to most investigations, bruises, abrasions, and contusions are by far the most common physical signs of abuse (Friedman & Morse, 1974; Holter & Friedman, 1968a; McRae *et al.*, 1973; Smith & Hanson, 1974). Bone fractures, head traumas, and subdural hematomas were found by these investigators also to be common in abused children. Ten to 15% of the children who suffered such injuries were reported in two of the studies to have later died (McRae *et al.*, 1973; Smith & Hanson, 1974), and one investigation suggests that between 8 and 10% of the injured children seen in pediatric emergency rooms may have injuries inflicted by their own parents (Holter & Friedman, 1968a).

It is important to recognize that episodes of child abuse do not always result in severe injuries that are treated in hospital emergency rooms; there is undoubtedly a large population of parents who physically harm their children, but do not leave such dramatic evidence of injury. Other parents may cause physical harm to their children but fail to seek out medical care for it. Since child abuse is usually diagnosed in the hospital setting due to the presence of nonaccidental physical injury, little is known about the types of injury sustained by abused children who are not seen in hospitals.

1.1.2. Distinctions among Child Abuse, Child Neglect, and Sexual Abuse

The phenomena of physical abuse, neglect, and sexual abuse are all forms of child maltreatment. They are often thought of as similar problems and suspected cases are usually investigated by a single child-protective service's agency. However, these types of child maltreatment actually appear quite different and may be relatively independent of one another.

As Friedman, Sandler, Hernandez, and Wolfe (1981) have pointed out, child abuse involves acts of *commission* by the parent, characterized by overt physical violence, beating, or excessive punishment. It is usually accompanied by anger or frustration toward the child, and occurs in discrete, often low-frequency episodes. On the other hand, child neglect involves maltreatment due to acts of *omission,* with the parent failing to meet a child's physical, nutritional, medical, emotional, and similar needs (Friedman *et al.*, 1981; Polansky, Hally, & Polansky, 1975). Rather than being episodic and discrete, neglect patterns are usually chronic and continual; rather than being associated with outbursts of parental anger, frustration, or hostility, neglectful parents often appear to be inattentive, indifferent, and unaware of their children's needs.

Sexual abuse occurring within families has received very little empirical attention within the child maltreatment literature; most reports to date have been anecdotal, descriptive, and based on uncontrolled case study sources. Sexual abuse in families has been defined as "the involvement of dependent, developmentally immature children and adolescents in sexual activities they do not fully comprehend . . . that violates the social taboos of family roles" (Schechter & Roberge, 1976). In contrast to the angry and punitive acts of abusive parents or the chronic indifference shown by neglectful parents, sexually exploitive parents are usually described as nonviolent toward the child but sexually and emotionally immature, seductive, and exhibiting difficulties in mature social/sexual relationships (Schechter & Roberge, 1976; Swanson, 1968).

While the area of family sexual exploitation is only beginning to receive research attention, there is little evidence to suggest that these parents are also likely to be aggressively abusive or neglectful toward their children. Similarly, physically abusive parents may or may not be simultaneously neglectful toward their children's basic needs. Because these maltreatment patterns probably have different causes, they may also require different intervention approaches and can best be considered as distinctive, although not always mutually exclusive, problems.

1.2. THE INCIDENCE OF CHILD ABUSE

Establishing the incidence of child abuse in this country is a very basic task, but it is one which has proven to be exceptionally difficult. One of the earliest incidence estimations was made by Gil (1970), who suggested that 6000 cases of child abuse occur annually. Later estimations were also higher; a report by the Education Commission of the States (1973) estimated that 60,000 children are abused each year. Other incidence data suggest that all of these figures are, in fact, substantial underestimations. Light's (1973) annual incidence rate is from 200,000 to 500,000 cases, while Helfer and Kempe (1976) note that 550,000 cases of suspected child abuse and neglect were reported in 1975.

A number of factors make it difficult to estimate accurately the incidence of child abuse:

Child abuse is a private act that, under most circumstances, cannot be directly assessed. Since professionals are not in a position to observe directly the private conduct of families, the existence of child-abusive behavior can be assessed only indirectly, such as when nonaccidental injury is diagnosed by a physician, when someone reports observing a family's child-abusive actions, or when parents themselves volunteer information that this is a problem which affects their family. The actual frequency of abuse undoubtedly far exceeds the number of cases "officially" detected in these ways.

Whether or not a family will be labeled as abusive is often based on the subjective judgment of professionals rather than on objective defining criteria. If a child sustains a physical injury that is clearly the result of intentional maltreatment by parents (such as multiple inflicted cigarette burns), professionals can reliably agree that abuse has occurred. However, other cases may not be assessed in so reliable a fashion. For example, if a child about to be spanked falls backward and strikes his head against a table, causing injury, this episode might (or might not) be considered evidence of abuse, depending on the interviewer's judgment (cf. Silver, 1968). Some children are disciplined by being hit on the buttocks with an object (such as a belt or a paddle) with sufficient force to leave marks for a short time. Whether such acts will be officially labeled as abusive, or instead considered as overly harsh but not really abusive discipline, often depends on an investigator's subjective judgment concerning the family. Thus, identifying and labeling families as child-abusive frequently involves matters of judgment rather than objective criteria. While this reliance on judgment is often necessary, it also makes incidence estimation less reliable.

Until recently, there was little uniformity across states concerning reporting procedures for suspected cases of child abuse. As reporting procedures have become more sophisticated and widely used, child abuse incidence estimations have also become more refined. Thus, what appears to be a greatly increased frequency of child abuse over the past ten years may be attributable to more accurate compilation of abuse reports and to an increased willingness of professionals and the public to report suspected cases.

Incidence estimates do not always take into account suspected versus documented cases and often fail to distinguish among physically abusive, sexually abusive, and neglectful behavior. The number of cases where physical abuse is *documented* is less than the number of cases where *suspicion* of abuse is reported. Further, since distinctions are not always made in the literature when reporting figures on abuse as opposed to neglect, accurate incidence figures for each are difficult to disentangle.

For all of these reasons, reports concerning the incidence of child abuse must be viewed cautiously and taken as estimates rather than objective, literal data. However, it is clear that as reporting–compilation procedures have become more refined and as both professionals and the general public have been made more aware of the problem, the frequency of reported instances of child abuse has also increased dramatically.

1.2.1. Violence Directed against Children: Results of One Normative Study

The most common method of estimating the scope of child-abusive behavior is determining the number of documented abuse cases within some geographic area and then extrapolating to the country at large, or determining the number of suspected cases that are reported to an agency which complies such reports (Cohen & Sussman, 1975). In order to yield accurate information, both of these approaches require that the abusive behavior shown by parents is observable. Since child abuse is usually not a public act and because the effects of a parent's abusive treatment toward the child are not always detected, these strategies do not reflect the actual prevalence of punitive child maltreatment.

An alternative approach for examining family behavior is assessing a normative sample of families to determine how often they make use of violent child-rearing practices. In one of the most comprehensive studies of this type, Gelles (1978) interviewed 1146 couples with children between the ages of three and seventeen. The families were selected by a national probability sampling procedure, and all families were interviewed with a standardized set of questions to determine the types of discipline they used with their children. The interview questions covered a variety of parental disciplinary practices that ranged in severity from spanking or slapping the child to much more violent acts such as kicking, biting, hitting, and beating up the youngster.

Table 1 summarizes some of the findings of the Gelles (1978) study, with data broken down based on the age of the child in the family. As the table indicates, the most common act of violence toward children of all ages was being slapped or spanked; 84% of youngsters three to four years old were reportedly spanked by their parents during the year prior to the interview. However, more extreme forms of parental violence also occurred at surprisingly high rates across the various age categories. Five percent of the parents of three- to four-year-olds reported throwing things at the child; 19.2% reported hitting the child with objects; 6.2% kicked, bit, or hit the child with a fist; and 1.1% of the parents surveyed reported "beating up" their three- to four-year-olds, defined by Gelles as delivering more than one punch to the youngster. Similar patterns are found for children of other ages as well.

Extrapolating these figures to the approximately 46 million children living with both parents in the 1975 survey year, Gelles (1978) suggests that between 1.0 and 1.9 million youngsters were kicked,

TABLE 1
Parent-to-Child Violence in Past Year by Age of Child[a]

Incident	Age of child (percent)			
	3–4 years	5–9 years	10–14 years	15–17 years
Threw something	5.1	7.0	3.6	5.1
Pushed/grabbed/shoved	39.0	39.1	27.9	20.8
Slapped or spanked	84.1	79.9	47.9	23.0
Kicked/bit/hit with fist	6.2	3.2	2.2	2.5
Hit with something	19.2	19.7	9.6	4.3
Beat up	1.1	0.9	1.1	1.7
Threatened with knife/gun	0.0	0.0	0.3	0.0
Used knife/gun	0.0	0.0	0.3	0.0

[a]Reprinted from Gelles (1978) with permission. From the *American Journal of Orthopsychiatry*. Copyright © 1978 by the American Orthopsychiatric Association, Inc.

bitten, or punched by their parents during that year; that 275,000–750,000 were "beaten up"; and that perhaps 46,000 children had a gun or knife "used" on them by their parents. Gelles notes that all of these figures may, in fact, represent underestimations, since these data were derived from interviews with parents, who would presumably be inclined to portray themselves in a socially desirable manner to an interviewer.

The Gelles (1978) study, although quite detailed, is subject to certain interpretational limitations. While practices such as "beating up" a child or "using a knife or gun" were somewhat operationalized, it is difficult to know exactly what specific behaviors parents referred to when they endorsed these interview items. The procedure is also limited by its reliance on retrospective reports by subjects of their own behavior, which do not necessarily correspond to the actual conduct of the parents over the past year. Extrapolating national incidence figures on parental violence from a sample of 1146 two-parent families has also been criticized, especially for those types of violence that occurred at very low rates in the study's sample (Pelton, 1979). Finally, and as Gelles (1978) points out, the aim of the project was to determine the frequency of violent acts directed by parents against their children, and not to assess whether this violence resulted in injury to the child. Thus, the investigation is not a direct survey of child abuse (which is a consequence of parental violence), but is rather a study of those acts by parents which might result in harm to the child. Even given these limitations, the results of this survey, taken together with incidence data on child abuse itself, indicate that violence directed toward children is a problem of major proportions in a surprisingly large number of American families.

1.3. SOCIOLEGAL PROCESSES IN THE HANDLING OF CHILD ABUSE CASES

Of the total number of parents who direct seriously violent aggression toward their children, a certain number will become officially designated as child-abusive parents. This labeling process is the result of not only the parent's act and the child's inflicted injury, but also a number of social and legal processes. Although exact procedures for handling cases of suspected child abuse vary from state to state, professionals should be aware of the general social and legal processes that affect abusive families.

In the past, there was great inconsistency across states concerning the reporting of suspected child abuse cases. This has changed, and states now have similar reporting statutes that apply to professionals (and often to the general public)*:

If evidence of child-abusive conduct by parents is found or if a child is suspected of being the victim of abuse, a professional must report this information to the agency responsible for investigating abuse. Most statutes do not require that an individual reporting a suspected case have physical documentation or otherwise *prove* that abuse occurred; only the professional's suspicion need be present for this reporting requirement to take effect. Mandatory reporting statutes take precedence over the normal confidentiality of a client–therapist relationship. Consequently, if one has reasonable suspicion that physical abuse of a child has occurred and if one does *not* report this suspicion to the appropriate child-protective agency, the individual failing to report the case is in violation of the child abuse reporting statute.

Professionals who report a case of suspected child abuse are generally protected from litigation concerning breach of confidentiality or if the abuse suspicion is found to be incorrect. The effect of this legal provision is to protect the individual who reports a suspected abuse case in the event that the child was not abused. It also protects the professional from litigation that could otherwise arise from breaking confidentiality (as might be alleged if a therapist makes a suspected abuse report that involved a patient). These protections do require that the report was made in good faith, e.g., with suspicion that child abuse occurred and without malice toward the parents.

*A review of every state's specific child abuse reporting statutes, investigative agencies, and procedures is beyond the scope of this book. Professionals who see cases of suspected abuse or neglect should always obtain information concerning their own state's current reporting laws and procedures and seek specific guidelines concerning their legal responsibilities and protection.

1.3.1. Steps That Are Ordinarily Followed in Cases of Suspected Child Abuse

After a report of suspected child maltreatment is received by a reporting agency, a series of investigative procedures generally take place. If there is evidence that the child was (or is being) seriously maltreated, additional legal and case treatment steps will follow. Figure 1 presents a schematic diagram of the process followed in most states.

Information concerning the suspected abuse case is routed to the local agency that investigates cases of child maltreatment. Suspicions of child abuse are initially reported in a variety of ways, including by telephone "hot lines," reports made to the police, and reports made by physicians or nurses to special child abuse teams in hospitals. This information is then directed to the child-protective agency under whose jurisdiction child abuse reports are investigated. The specific agency that investigates such reports varies from state to state, but is often a child-protective services division of the local welfare department. When the initial information has been received by this agency, an investigation is then conducted.

The suspected case of child abuse is investigated. In this data-gathering phase, agency caseworkers attempt to determine whether the child is a victim of maltreatment and, if so, to assess the seriousness of the situation. Information on the child's injury or physical condition is obtained; parents, the child, professionals, and others who are familiar with the family are interviewed. When this information has been reviewed, the agency reaches some judgment concerning the case. If the investigation does not indicate the child is abused or neglected, the case is closed at this point. On the other hand, if there is evidence of maltreatment, additional actions will follow. What those steps are, and how quickly they are taken, largely depends upon the seriousness of the family's problems and the likelihood of danger to the child.

Case follow-up is provided by the protective services agency. If a family is in need of continued contact or counseling, but the child is not felt to be seriously at risk of harm, case follow-up may be provided by the

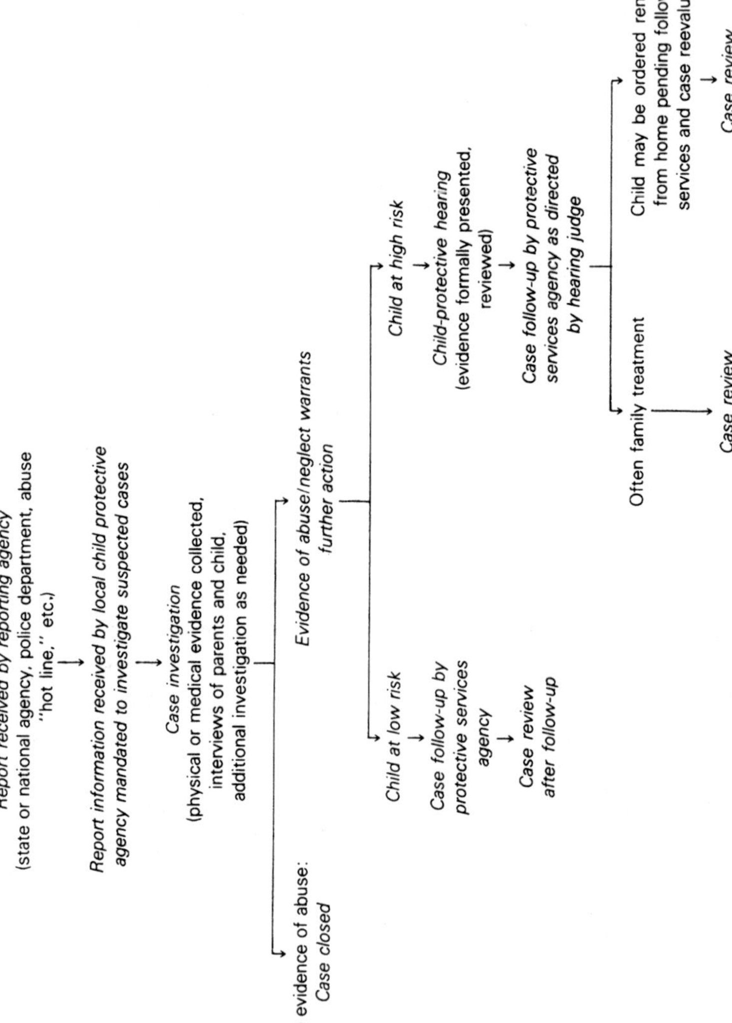

FIGURE 1. A typical handling of suspected child abuse cases.

agency for some period of time. Basic social services, counseling, or referral of the family for more specific forms of assistance is often provided.

A formal child-protective hearing is held to evaluate the child's well-being and safety. If the agency investigation indicates the possibility of a more serious situation, a formal hearing is conducted to review the agency's findings and arrive at a plan to ensure the child's physical safety. Hearings of this type are usually conducted before a juvenile or family court judge, with both child-protective agency staff and the family present. The hearing's purpose is usually not to consider possible criminal evidence, but instead to order whatever steps are needed to protect the child.

If the court finds that a youngster has been maltreated, any of several actions may be directed. Judges can order the family to receive counseling services, either provided by the child-protective caseworker or by some other agency. If the child is felt to be at serious risk, temporary foster care placement and removal of parental custody can be implemented until the family is able to meet the child's safety needs. A plan for the periodic review of progress in the case is also usually specified by the judge.

The entire process described here is essentially a protective–remedial one, with the court directing (and a designated agency coordinating) steps to protect the child and to improve those conditions which led to the youngster's past harm. If a family is consistently uncooperative over a long period of time and if the child would be at risk if ever returned home, a court can permanently terminate parental rights. If a child is seriously injured in an intentional manner, criminal charges can also be brought against the parents through separate legal channels. These, however, are relatively unusual outcomes that agencies and courts seek to avoid except in the most extreme cases.

1.4. THE ROLE OF MENTAL HEALTH PROFESSIONALS IN TREATING CHILD-ABUSIVE FAMILIES

When a child-abusive family has come to the attention of child-protective authorities, the overall and usual case management objective is to make the family environment safe for the child. Almost invariably, this will include providing therapy and other counseling services to family members, and in particular to the parents.

Mental health workers become involved in treating child-abusive families in several ways. In some cases, the child-protective caseworker who has contact with a family during the initial abuse investigation phase will remain responsible for that family's intervention and will be the primary provider of treatment. In other cases, a family will be referred by the child-protective agency to some other facility for specialized services. If this kind of referral takes place, the staff of a mental health center, child and family clinic, community counseling service, or similar facility may become responsible for providing treatment to the abusive family. Social workers, psychologists, psychiatrists, and other types of therapists are all called upon to intervene with these families, and we will consider intervention approaches in detail later in this book. However, it will be useful first to review some of the clinical research on abusive parents and abused children and to integrate these findings into a conceptual framework that can be used to guide the treatment of child-abusive families.

2

Characteristics of Abusive Parents and Abused Children

In any area of science, and certainly in the study of human behavior, there is a series of progressive steps that characterize our level of understanding of a phenomenon. The first and most basic step toward understanding a behavioral problem is being able to describe it. Once we are able to describe accurately the characteristics of the problem or phenomenon, we can then develop a theoretical or conceptual model to account for what is observed. Finally, based on an adequate conceptual model, it is possible to generate specific predictions and interventions concerning the problem in which we are interested.

In the case of child abuse, being able to describe characteristics of abusive parents and abused children can provide us with important information that is ultimately related to our formulations about the causes of this problem and its treatment. Within the child abuse literature over the past 15 years, a large number of studies have examined characteristics of abusive families. The purpose of this chapter is to review some of the major findings of these studies and to consider, in at least some cases, their methodological adequacy.

2.1. PARENT CHARACTERISTICS ASSOCIATED WITH ABUSIVE BEHAVIOR

The earliest studies of abusive parents were based, almost entirely, on anecdotal reports drawn from very limited clinical samples. Investigators gradually began to use more quantified methods to study parent and family factors related to child abuse and, still later, a number of projects using control group comparisons appeared in the literature. While many different variables related to abuse have been proposed, attention has focused most extensively on several: socioeconomic factors (especially those which create life stress for the family); deficits in the parent's knowledge and use of appropriate child-management skills; lack of knowledge concerning "normal" child behavior; a parent's history of having also been raised in an abusive family environment; social isolation; parent personality disorders; family discord and stress; and emotional overreactivity when the child misbehaves or emits other aversive behavior.

2.1.1. Socioeconomic Disadvantage

A large number of investigators have proposed a relationship between socioeconomic disadvantage and patterns of child maltreatment. Gil (1970; 1975), for example, has argued that the deprivations of poverty, including high-density living in deteriorating housing, few financial resources, large numbers of children, the absence of child care alternatives, single-parent households, and inadequate social support services, create chronic stress and frustration for the economically disadvantaged family. This level of pervasive life-style frustration, according to Gil (1975), creates a "triggering context" in which violence toward children is more likely to occur. While Gil emphasizes that poverty per se is not a direct cause of child abuse, the stress and lack of support resources which characterize extreme social disadvantage can reduce a parent's general adaptability and self-control, thereby increasing the likelihood of family violence. In similar fashion, Gelles (1973) suggests that "structural" social stressors such as unemployment and large family size without adequate economic resources, as well as values or norms favoring the appropriateness of physical punishment, are factors which precipitate patterns of violence within the family.

Several investigators have reported that indices of socioeconomic disadvantage occur disproportionately more often in abusive families. Gil (1970), in a study of a large population of abusive parents, found that the sample's mean educational level, income, and occupational status were lower than those of the general population. Garbarino (1976) examined such ecological factors as population transience, unemployment, income, educational background, and family standard of living in relation to frequency of reported child abuse in 58 counties in New York state. The investigator found that a substantial proportion of the variance (36%) in rates of reported child abuse across the counties could be accounted for by measures of socioeconomic stress and the absence of adequate support systems. In a later project, Garbarino and Sherman (1980) concluded that the "social impoverishment" of communities (defined in terms of poor appearance, housing quality, social support networks, neighborhood public image, and community resources) is more strongly related to patterns of child maltreatment than is low socioeconomic level per se.

Surveys of families adjudicated as child-abusive find that the parents are often from low-socioeconomic-status (SES) groups and have chronic economic and social problems associated with impoverishment (cf. Giovannoni & Billingsley, 1970; Pelton, 1978). While these studies generally rely on large-scale demographic survey analysis, at least one recent comparison group project found that a major predictor which distinguishes neglectful from normal control families is socioeconomic stress (Gaines, Sandgrund, Green, & Power, 1978). Interestingly, while abusive parents scored high in life stressors, the largest differences were obtained between neglectful and normal parents.

However, not all investigations have yielded unequivocal evidence concerning the relationship between social disadvantage and child abuse. In a comparison of 134 physically abused children with 53 nonabused children, Smith and his associates (Smith & Hanson, 1974; Smith, Hanson, & Noble, 1974) did find group differences on such measures as adequacy of family living residence and parent income. However, when equated for a social class discrepancy that had existed between the groups, most of the individual SES variables no longer differentiated abusive from control families. Steele and Pollock (1968), in yet another project, have described the occurrence of child-abusive patterns among upper- and middle-class families.

Limitations of Inferences about Socioeconomic Status and Child Abuse. Many studies examining SES factors in relation to child abuse find evidence that reported child maltreatment is correlated with social and economic stress. While most investigators are careful to avoid inferring a direct causal relationship between poverty and child abuse, the life stressors of families living with only marginal social and economic supports can be conducive to the development of frustration and violence, including child maltreatment. This certainly does not mean that child abuse is limited to families subjected to socioeconomic stress, nor that most families under even severe SES stress abuse their children. It only indicates that the reported frequency of child maltreatment appears to be associated with indices of social and economic disadvantage.

One potential methodological bias in studies of socioeconomic status should be noted. Presumably, families with limited economic resources are likely to use the services of community clinics, charity hospitals, and similar public agencies for their health care and social service needs, while affluent families are more likely to see private practitioners. It is possible that public agencies or clinics are more likely to recognize and report cases of suspected child abuse to welfare authorities than are the private practitioners who treat middle- and upper-class families. If this occurs, it would bias a study's sample with an overrepresentation of low-SES families whose abuse is either more detectable or more likely to be reported to authorities than the abuse of high-SES families.

2.1.2. A Parent's Own History of Having Been Abused

One of the most frequently cited characteristics of abusive parents is that they, as children, were the targets of violence from their own parents. This finding has been reported in anecdotal case studies and descriptive reports (Silver, 1968; Silver, Dublin, & Lourie, 1969;

Wasserman, 1967) as well as descriptions based on larger survey samples of abusive parents (Bell, 1973; Green, 1976; Green, Gaines, & Sandgrund, 1974). Investigators have interpreted the relationship between a parent's history of childhood abuse and the parent's current abusive behavior toward his or her own child in various ways, including psychoanalytically (e.g., a failure to identify with a "mothering" role and an anger at one's own parents directed instead toward one's child) and behaviorally (e.g., imitatively learning the violent child-management practices exhibited by one's own parents).

While the notion that abusive parents were themselves abused as children is widely accepted, there have actually been surprisingly few well-controlled empirical studies of this question (Berger, 1980). In one controlled investigation, Spinetta (1978) administered to groups of abusive and nonabusive mothers a self-report measure that included items about the respondent's childhood relationship with her own parents. Abusive parents in this study reported that they had a significantly poorer relationship with their own parents than did control group subjects, although the question of whether they had been physically abused was not directly scrutinized.

Reports that abusive parents experienced violence in their own childhood are extremely common in the literature, but are rarely based on controlled investigations. While violent upbringing may be common in the background of abusive parents, there are undoubtedly a large number of *non*abusive parents who were exposed to similar patterns of family violence when they were young. Causal relationships based primarily on characteristics observed in a clinical population must be regarded as tentative until well-controlled comparative studies are undertaken.

2.1.3. Social Isolation

Social isolation of the parent is another frequently cited characteristic of child-abusive families (Green, 1976; Helfer, 1973; Holmes, Barnhart, Cantoni, & Reymer, 1975; Parke & Collmer, 1975; Smith *et al.*, 1974; Spinetta, 1978). All of these writers indicate that abusive parents often have relatively few close friends, lack interpersonal sources of emotional support, experience loneliness, and are uninvolved in close social relationships outside the home. The clinical picture described in these reports suggests a parent with few social gratifications to meet her or his own needs, together with the feeling of being "trapped" alone at home with the child.

While this conclusion rests largely on anecdotal evidence and on studies using nonstringent control groups, other investigators have established more definitive relationships between parent social isolation and parent–child difficulties in the home. Wahler and his colleagues (Wahler, 1980; Wahler, Leske, & Rogers, 1979) describe what they term the "insular mother," an individual whose low-frequency interactions with others are often aversive and are rarely with persons whom the parent thinks of as friends. This is in contrast to the interaction pattern of noninsular parents, who not only have greater social contact with others but whose interactions are more likely to be positive in nature and to occur with people regarded as friends. In an initial study, Wahler *et al.* (1979) found that parents who did not benefit from a child-management training program were those who could be described as insular, whereas success and maintained improvement after parent training were related to an individual's frequency of positive social contacts with friends. In a later project, Wahler (1980) used an in-the-home observational procedure to analyze the parent–child interactions of mothers who were insular and were also receiving training in child-management techniques. The study found that the frequency of contacts a mother had with friends was inversely related to the number of problems she had at home with her child and her own skill in dealing with them. Further, on individual days when a parent had increased social contacts with others, her interactions with the child were also more positive.

Taken together, the findings of social isolation among abusive parents and the more recent research on insularity suggest that the quality and quantity of a parent's relationships with others outside the family can influence parent–child interactions occurring in the home. While the basis for this pattern has not been empirically established, it may well involve a decrease in parents' general adaptability and effectiveness (and an increase in frustration) when they experience few gratifications in their own social relationships.

2.1.4. Parent Personality Characteristics

One of the most widely investigated questions in the child abuse literature is whether stable personality characteristic differences exist between abusive and nonabusive parents and, if so, what those characteristics are (cf. review articles by Berger, 1980; Shorkey, 1978; Spinetta & Rigler, 1972). Unfortunately, the number of studies in this area appear to far exceed the definitiveness of their conclusions. However, we can direct our attention to three types of issues involving the personality characteristics of abusive parents. These are the incidence of severe psychopathology among abusers, case study inferences concerning the personality characteristics of abusive parents, and efforts to establish typologies of child-abusive individuals.

2.1.4.1. Severe Psychopathology among Child-Abusive Parents

Early descriptive reports on child abuse argued that overt parental maltreatment of children was frequently associated with parental sociopathy and psychosis (cf. Cochrane, 1965; Miller, 1959; Woolley and Evans, 1955). As studies of abusive families grew in scale, it became apparent that the incidence of demonstrable psychopathology among these parents had been overestimated. Most investigators now estimate that only a relatively small percentage (usually considered to be 5–10%) of abuse cases involve parents who can be diagnosed as psychotic, schizophrenic, or sociopathic (Bell, 1973; Friedman *et al.*, 1981; Kempe, 1973; Kempe & Kempe, 1978; Steele & Pollock, 1968).

2.1.4.2. Descriptive Reports of Parent Personality Characteristics

A large number of studies have explored personality traits felt to characterize child-abusive parents and, presumably, to cause abusive behavior. Some of these projects involve making inferences drawn only from a clinical sample of several experimentally uncontrolled case descriptions (cf. Blumberg, 1974; Silver *et al.*, 1969; Wasserman, 1967). Other projects are based on structured personality assessment interviews with larger abusive parent samples (Bell, 1973; Green, 1976; Green *et al.*, 1974; Smith, Hanson, & Noble, 1973), although rigorous control group comparisons clearly remain the exception, rather than the rule, in this literature. For the most part, descriptive personality characteristic studies rely on psychoanalytic conceptualizations of personality.

Those personality variables most frequently attributed to abusive parents include: *poor impulse control, low frustration tolerance, and difficulties expressing anger appropriately* (Green, 1976; Kempe *et al.*, 1962; Steele & Pollock, 1968; Wasserman, 1967); *low self-esteem and feelings of insufficiency* (Bell, 1973; Blumberg, 1974; Green *et al.*, 1974); *emotional immaturity* (Boisvert, 1972; Holter & Friedman, 1968b; Steele & Pollock, 1968); and a *rigid, inflexible personality style* (Holter & Friedman, 1968; Merrill, 1962; Steele & Pollock, 1968). A phenomenon termed *role reversal* has also been observed among abusive individuals; this refers to the parent's unrealistic tendency to expect the child to be a source of social or emotional support and companionship, a reversal of the appropriate role in which the parent meets the young child's needs (Blumberg, 1974; Green, 1976; Green *et al.*, 1974; Helfer, 1973). Presumably, because a child is not able to meet the unrealistic expectations of the parent, the parent in turn becomes frustrated, hostile, and finally abusive toward the youngster.

Based on these observations, investigators began to propose more systematic abusive parent personality typologies and to assess whether personality differences between abusive and nonabusive parents could be empirically detected.

2.1.4.3. Typologies and Structured Personality Assessment

One of the earliest and most widely cited attempts at describing types of child abusers based on personality variables is the categorization proposed by Merrill (1962). According to Merrill's formulation, one of three distinctive personality patterns can be observed in most abusive fathers and mothers. The first personality type involves the presence of hostility and aggression triggered by ordinary difficulties and frustrations. A second and different type of abusive parent is characterized by excessive rigidity, compulsiveness, and a lack of warmth toward the child. Finally, Merrill (1962) suggests that a third abusive personality pattern involves extreme passivity, dependency, and immaturity. Following Merrill's early attempt at descriptive personality classification, other investigators outlined typologies that involve what are essentially similar characteristics (Boisvert, 1972; Delsordo, 1963; Zalba, 1967; Knight, Disbrow, & Doerr, 1978). It is important to note, however, that these personality categorization systems are based almost entirely on general, intuitive clinical impressions from limited case samples rather than objective, well-validated criteria.

If personality characteristics of abusive and nonabusive parents are evaluated using more objective, standardized measures, can differences be found? Several investigators have administered the Minnesota Multiphasic Personality Inventory (MMPI) to abusive and control parents (Paulson, Afifi, Thomason, & Chaleef, 1974; Wright, 1976), but these studies largely failed to detect statistically significant MMPI clinical scale differences between the groups. Other projects yielded similarly equivocal findings, with either few personality differences found or with inconsistent patterns across personality test measures (Floyd, 1975; Gaines *et al.*, 1978; Wright, 1976). One of the few well-controlled studies that has found differences between abusive and nonabusive parents was reported by Spinetta (1978), who administered the Minnesota Screening Profile of Parenting (Helfer, Schneider, & Hoffmeister, 1977) to groups of child-abusive mothers and control subjects. Abusive parents were found to score higher than nonabusive parents from the same SES level in the tendencies to become upset and angry, to feel isolated and lonely, and to fear external threat and control.

2.1.4.4. *Limitations of Personality Characteristic Studies of Child Abusers*

Attempting to identify parent personality correlates associated with child-abusive behavior has been the subject of a large number of writers. Unfortunately, there is a striking paucity of well-controlled empirical research in this area; many of the widely held assumptions concerning the personality makeup of child-abusive parents are based upon casual descriptive observation rather than controlled studies. For the most part, these personality explorations have failed to utilize matched control groups, quantified and validated assessment instruments, and operationalized, testable constructs (Berger, 1980; Gelles, 1973). While certain personality characteristics (such as difficulties in anger control and poor response to frustration) are frequently attributed to child-abusive parents, these descriptors are somewhat unilluminating and redundant given that the parent is already known to have directed violence toward his or her child. A major conclusion we can reach is that there is currently little empirical evidence to support the existence of a clear child abuse personality "type" and, following from this, it does not appear possible to predict whether an individual is a child abuser based on personality characteristics.

2.1.5. Family Discord and Intrafamily Stress

As we discussed earlier, it has been suggested that socioeconomic stress can function as a "triggering" context factor for child abuse. However, apart from socially or economically stressful external conditions, other investigators have proposed that stressors *within* the family may also contribute to abusive behavior. The effects of marital discord, large family size, and family frustration due to unemployment have received the greatest amount of attention in this regard.

Several studies report that single-parent households are more common among child-abusive families than among nonabusive families. Ebbin, Gollub, Stein, and Wilson (1969) found that only 30% of their study's abusive parents had intact marriages compared to 53% of control group families. Elmer (1977) reported similar differences in the frequency of intact marriages between abusive and nonabusive families, while other investigators have cited an overrepresentation of one-parent households among abusers (Gil, 1970; Nurse, 1964; Smith *et al.*, 1974; Young, 1964). For couples whose relationship is intact, there is evidence that marital discord (spouse arguments, physical violence, and lack of emotional support) is a relatively frequent problem (Bennie & Sclare, 1969; Green *et al.*, 1974; Ory & Earp, 1980; Smith, 1975; Young, 1964). While the functional relationship of such marital factors to child abuse is not always described, one can speculate that families headed by one parent may be susceptible to greater internal stress (due to the single parent's multiple responsibilities and the lack of available support from a spouse) and that maritally discordant couples experience greater emotional frustration, an increased likelihood of resolving conflicts through argument, less mutual emotional support, and fewer opportunities for collaborative problem-solving.

Large family size itself may be a source of internal family stress, with several reports indicating that abusive parents have more children than nonabusive families (Gil, 1970; Light, 1973; Young, 1964). When we consider that parental unemployment appears to occur more often in child-abusive households (Gelles, 1973; Gil, 1970), there is evidence that some of these families may have the responsibility not only of caring for more children, but also of doing so with fewer financial resources.

2.1.6. Lack of Knowledge about Children

When parent personality variables were reviewed, we noted that investigators have described the phenomenon of "role reversal" among abusers. Most theorists have interpreted an abusive parent's efforts to derive need satisfaction from his or her child as an indication of an underlying personality disturbance related to the parent's emotional immaturity (Blumberg, 1974; Green *et al.*, 1974; Wasserman, 1967). However, an alternative and perhaps simpler explanation is that abusive parents lack everyday knowledge concerning what to expect of children and therefore have unrealistic expectations concerning their own children's conduct. If this is the case, the parent could become frustrated because the child does not yet have the developmental capability of responding in the manner the parent inappropriately expects.

Several investigators have concluded that child behaviors which elicit abusive parental responses are often actions which are considered normal for youngsters at that age or developmental level (Friedman *et al.*, 1981; Scott, 1973; Weston, 1968). In addition, there are widespread descriptive reports that child-abusive parents have little practical knowledge concerning the developmental behavioral competencies of youngsters (Elmer, 1977; Galdston, 1965; Smith & Hanson, 1975; Spinetta & Rigler, 1972); one welfare agency survey found that 19% of abusive parents had inappropriate developmental expectations concerning their own children (Report of the Iowa Department of Social Services, cited in Berger, 1980). Taken together, these findings suggest that abusive parents may lack practical knowledge of child development and behavior and attribute overly advanced behavioral maturity to their children.

2.1.7. Child-Management Skill Deficits

Closely related to the question of whether abusive parents know what to expect of children is the even more relevant issue of whether they are able to manage, control, and interact with their youngsters appropriately. This is a very fundamental question; on the face of it, one would suspect that abusive parents may behave abusively because they lack the skills to handle their children's behavior in a nonviolent manner. In this regard, it is somewhat surprising that close attention to abusive parents' child-management skills is a very recent development.

While much of the traditional psychopathology-oriented literature assumes that abusive parents intentionally seek to injure their children, child-management research postulates that abusive individuals often behave violently and punitively because they do not know how to handle child misbehavior in appropriate ways (Crozier & Katz, 1979; Doctor & Singer, 1978; Friedman *et al.*, 1981). Evidence to support a child-management skill deficit conceptualization can be found in a number of systematic case study analyses in which the behavior of abusive parents toward their children was directly observed during interactions in the home or in a clinic setting (Crimmins, Bradlyn, St. Lawrence, & Kelly, 1982; Crozier & Katz, 1979; Denicola & Sandler, 1980; Sandler, Van Dercar, & Milhoan, 1978; Scott, Baer, Christoff, & Kelly, 1982; Wolfe & Sandler, 1981; Wolfe, St. Lawrence, Graves, Brehony, Bradlyn, & Kelly, 1982). While the specific parent skill variables under observation differ across these studies, all found evidence that abusive parents exhibit low rates of positive and appropriate behavior when interacting with their children (such as praising desirable child conduct, showing physical affection, and conveying requests clearly) and often display high rates of ineffective behavior (failing to notice the child's good actions, threatening punishment, or making unclear and inconsistent commands). Several investigations also indicate that the parents experience difficulty handling their children's misbehavior at home, and that attempts to control misbehaviors through punishment led to injury to the youngster in the past (Mastria, Mastria, & Harkins, 1979; Wolfe & Sandler, 1981; Wolfe *et al.*, 1982).

While the close behavioral assessment of child-management skill deficits undertaken in these projects suggests that abusive parents do not interact skillfully with their children and do not handle child misbehaviors effectively, the studies are limited because they rest primarily on single case demonstrations. A larger and more systematic identification of child-management deficits has been undertaken by Burgess and Conger (Burgess, 1979; Burgess & Conger, 1977a, b, 1978). Groups of abusive, neglectful, and normal families were matched on socioeconomic, family structure, and educational levels and were recruited to participate in a project to assess their family interaction patterns. Trained observers in each subject's home used a behavioral observation coding system to rate the families' interaction during three types of staged interaction task: competitive games, cooperative games, and family discussions. Total observation time in the home averaged six hours (or 1500 separate observation intervals) per family, and a variety of positive and negative behaviors, both verbal and physical, were coded during the observation sessions.

Burgess and Conger found several consistent differences between abusive and control parents when they were observed in their own homes. Perhaps the most important finding involves the frequency of positive and negative actions directed by parents toward their children. Abusive mothers displayed 40% *fewer* positive behaviors (such as affection and supportive comments) toward their children during the interaction tasks than control group mothers, but displayed 60% *higher* rates of negative actions (such as complaints and threats) than the nonabusive mothers (Burgess, 1979; Burgess & Conger, 1978). Neglectful parents interacted in a manner similar to the abusive mothers, but with even lower rates of positive behaviors and higher rates of negative behaviors than their abusive counterparts. Thus, the results of these carefully controlled projects indicate that child-abusive parents underutilize positive types of social-interaction skills with their children and use, to a greater extent than nonabusive parents, negative and threatening actions when dealing with their youngsters in everyday situations.

There are two related issues to consider with respect to the study of parent–child interaction behavior within child-abusive families. One issue is how abusive parents and their children behave during ordinary, everyday, routine interactions. A second and somewhat different matter is how the parent handles the less ordinary and more serious behavior problems exhibited by his or her child. Some projects have shown that abusive parents interact in a negative and inattentive manner during casual, routine situations with their children (Burgess & Conger, 1977b, 1978; Crimmins *et al.*, 1982). At the same time, many abusive individuals appear also to lack the appropriate management skills that are needed to control their children's misbehaviors without violence (Mastria *et al.*, 1979; Wolfe & Sandler, 1981; Wolfe *et al.*, 1982). This would suggest that there may be two different, but related, forms of interaction deficit among abusive parents: those skills needed to interact positively and attentively with a child during everyday situations and those skills needed to handle or control a child's misbehavior in a nonviolent manner.

2.1.8. Emotional Overreactivity to the Child's Misbehavior

A very common observation in the child abuse literature is that abusive parents feel a sense of arousal, anger, frustration, and loss of control during the period preceding an abuse episode (Bennie & Sclare, 1969; Blumberg, 1974; Nurse, 1964; Wasserman, 1967). These clinical descriptions suggest the possibility that abusive parents become emotionally overaroused and overreactive in certain situations involving their children, and that this overreactivity (especially if it takes the form of anger or feelings of loss of control) contributes to the onset of abusive acts.

Recent investigations have examined the physiological reactions of abusive parents to cues of child positive behavior and misbehavior. Disbrow, Doerr, and Caulfield (1977) compared the responses of abusing, neglecting, and normal parents to videotapes which showed positive, negative, and neutral family interactions. Physiological assessment showed that while the heart rate of normal parents varied with the type of family interaction they were observing, abusive and neglectful parents demonstrated little variation in heart rate across the types of scenes and were generally more aroused throughout the session.

In a similar paradigm, Frodi and Lamb (1980) had abusive mothers and a matched group of nonabusive mothers watch videotapes of crying and smiling infants. During the observation sessions, physiological signs of arousal (heart rate, diastolic blood pressure, and skin conductance) were continuously monitored and subjects were asked to describe their emotional reactions following each infant-crying or infant-smiling scene. While both abusive and nonabusive parents showed signs of heightened physiological arousal to the videotape of an infant crying, abusers showed a greater increase in their heart rate reactivity than did the controls. Abusers also described greater annoyance at the cry stimulus than their nonabusive counterparts. When watching the smiling infant, control group parents showed little change from their normal state of physiological activation; abusive parents, in contrast, showed arousal even to the scenes of a smiling infant.

Finally, Wolfe, Fairbank, Kelly, and Bradlyn (in press) analyzed patterns of arousal for abusive and nonabusive mothers as they watched videotapes showing children behaving well (for example, complying with an adult's requests or playing) and the same child misbehaving (crying or shouting "no" when given a direction). Abusive parents showed greater arousal, as assessed by skin conductance, during the misbehavior scenes and remained more aroused, based on respiration responses, when they watched both types of scenes.

While research in this area is still preliminary, these projects provide physiological assessment evidence which collaborates clinical reports that abusive parents are stressed during certain interactions with their children. These individuals appear to respond in a more aroused manner than nonabusive parents to portrayals of child misbehavior or to aversive cues like crying, and they seem to respond in a more aroused fashion even to neutral or positive portrayals of child conduct.

2.1.9. Conclusions and Summary of Abusive Parent Characteristic Research

As we have seen, a number of different factors have been proposed as possible contributors to child-abusive behavior. These include social stresses, primarily the pressures experienced by those low in SES and inadequately served by community resources, as well as personal intrafamily stressors, including marital discord or breakup, large family size, and unemployment. All of these factors have been found to occur more often among child-abusive families, although this pattern may be biased if low-SES abusers are more likely to be detected than high-SES abusers.

Efforts to identify stable personality characteristics of abusive parents, although the subject of much discussion in the literature, have yielded few firm, empirically validated conclusions. For the most part, the personality traits most often attributed to abusive parents (e.g., having poor impulse control, experiencing aggression control difficulties) do not seem to *explain* the causes of abusive behavior so much as they simply *describe* the abusive act. Thus, while a small percentage of child-abusing parents exhibit clear-cut psychopathology (psychosis or sociopathic disorders), attempts to establish abusive personality "types" have been generally unsuccessful.

Current research suggests that abusive parents do have certain situational deficits and problems. One of them is social isolation, with many of these parents reporting few sources of positive, gratifying contact with others around them. Presumably, if they are isolated from others, they are also isolated from sources of everyday information concerning child and child rearing. A second problem is in the area of child-management and child-interaction skills. A number of recent controlled case studies and group comparison projects have shown that abusive parents often lack the skills repertoire to interact effectively with their children on an everyday basis, to manage child misbehaviors nonviolently, and to use positive means of dealing with child problems. Finally, preliminary but well-controlled research indicates that abusive parents react in a more physiologically aroused, and presumably more stressed, manner than nonabusive parents to their children in general and to aversive behavior by children in particular.

2.2. CHARACTERISTICS OF ABUSED CHILDREN

Understandably, most studies of child abuse have focused greatest attention on the parent since it is the parent who is the perpetrator of the violent act. However, there is a growing recognition that parent–child interactions involve behavioral reciprocity, with the child also influencing the parent's conduct (Bell, 1968; Milow & Lourie, 1964). Thus, attention has been directed toward identifying characteristics of children that are associated with either a risk for, or history of, abuse.

A frequent observation is that abused children exhibit behavior problems more frequently than nonabused children and, consequently, their parents experience more difficulty managing the youngster (Friedrich & Boriskin, 1976; Green, 1976; Helfer, 1973; McRae *et al.*, 1973; Milow & Lourie, 1964). In addition to general child unmanageability as reported by the parent, investigators have specifically noted an increased incidence of hyperactivity (Baldwin & Oliver, 1975; Friedrich & Boriskin, 1976; Helfer, 1973; Johnson & Morse, 1968; McRae *et al.*, 1973), irritability and colic (Baldwin & Oliver, 1975; Friedrich & Boriskin, 1976; Milow & Lourie, 1964), and coordination or physical handicaps (Friedrich & Boriskin, 1976; Helfer, 1973; Johnson & Morse, 1968) among abused children.

The intellectual level of the child has also been a subject of investigation in several studies, with abused children reported to have lower IQ test scores than nonabused children. Smith and Hanson (1974), for example, found that their sample of abused youngsters achieved a mean IQ score of 89, relative to a nonabused control group's average score of 97. Other investigators have found a higher-than-expected incidence of mental retardation among abused children (Elmer & Gregg, 1967; Friedrich & Boriskin, 1976; Martin, Beezley, Conway, & Kempe, 1974; Morse, Sahler, & Friedman, 1970), although this pattern has not been replicated in all studies (Report of the Iowa Department of Social Services, cited in Berger, 1980).

A final characteristic that has been associated with increased risk for abuse is prematurity of birth (Elmer & Gregg, 1967; Fontana, 1973; Friedrich & Boriskin, 1976; McRae *et al.*, 1973). While the reason for a relationship between infant prematurity and abuse has not been closely evaluated, Burgess (1979) has suggested that premature infants are more likely to exhibit developmental difficulties and speculated that the hospital procedures typically followed for premature infants may interfere with normal social bonding and attachment between the mother and child.

All of these characteristics can be interpreted to support the contention that children who are abused are usually difficult to manage and "pull" abusive responses from the parent. A child who exhibits serious behavior problems, is developmentally handicapped, is hyperactive, or is continually irritable may be unresponsive to his parent's routine attempts at child management and, in fact, may elicit increasingly punitive actions by the parent. However, it is important to note that research to date has not established such a direction of causality; it is equally possible that abusive parents, either by their style of parenting or by a lack of concern for their child's development, contribute to a child's developmental and behavior problems. Clearly, this is an area where additional research is needed.

3

A Social-Learning Model of Child Abuse

As we pointed out earlier, describing a behavioral phenomenon such as child abuse represents only the first level or our knowledge about it. The next step is to integrate what is known about abuse into a conceptual model that suggests specific forms of intervention for abusive families. However, before exploring such a model, several limiting factors should be noted. First, any sound conceptual framework must be built upon a foundation of accurate descriptive data. As we saw in the preceding chapter, the number of *well-controlled* studies of child-abusive families remains relatively small. Of necessity, any present conceptual model of child abuse must rely in part on clinically derived, rather than rigorously validated, sources of information about abusive families. As we continue to learn more about these families, efforts to explain, predict, and control child abuse can become correspondingly more refined and rigorous. This, in turn, leads to a second issue. Conceptual models, including those of child abuse, should be capable not only of accounting for our current knowledge of a problem, but also of generating testable new predictions. Ultimately, a model of the kind presented in this chapter is useful to the extent that it stimulates additional avenues for child abuse research and applied treatment.

3.1. TRADITIONAL FORMULATION OF CHILD ABUSE

Traditional theories to account for child abuse have stressed the operation of broad, single-factor causes. Historically, the two models which have received the greatest attention are the *psychiatric model* and the *sociological model* of child abuse (see critical reviews by Belsky, Burgess, 1979; and 1978; Parke and Collmer, 1975).

The psychiatric model postulates that child-abusive behavior results largely from internal emotional disturbances of the parent, as well as personality traits which permit the parent to engage in abusive activity. Almost certainly, the origin of this theoretical model was the assumption that no one other than a "sick person" could be violent toward a child. Therefore, understanding child abuse required one to first understand the more basic psychopathology of the parent.

As we noted in Chapter 2, a small percentage of abusive parents do exhibit demonstrable emotional disorders and can, for example, be reliably classified as psychotic or sociopathic. However, as one moves away from these clear-cut but relatively infrequent cases, evidence for a psychopathology-based model of child abuse becomes much less adequate. Recent criticisms of the psychiatric model note: (1) an absence of well-controlled research supporting the contention that most abusive parents can be diagnosed as suffering from definitive emotional disorders; (2) the failure to operationalize and define clearly the types of disorders or characteristics that produce child abuse; and (3) the failure to take into account systematically the role of external situational factors, such as social stress, child-management deficits, and other coping skill inadequacies (Berger, 1980; Burgess, 1979; Gelles, 1973).

In contrast to the psychiatric model of abuse, sociological theories account for child abuse by emphasizing the impact of socioeconomic stress on parents and families. According to this viewpoint, a variety of stressors caused by social and economic disadvantage (including poverty, unemployment, limited community support resources, inadequate child care facilities, and large family size) create a climate in which child abuse, as well as other forms of violence, develop. The major support for a sociological theory of abuse rests with correlational–demographic studies showing relationships between abuse reports and SES indices; some of these reports were summarized in Chapter 2. The major limitation of this model is that it does not explain why the great majority of families, even those under chronic and extreme socioeconomic disadvantage, do *not* abuse their children. In similar fashion, while correlational relationships between SES measures and child abuse have been reported, there is no clear evidence to document that these relationships are, in fact, directly causal.

As several investigators have pointed out (Belsky, 1978; Burgess & Conger, 1978; Parke & Collmer, 1975), both psychiatric and sociological explanations of child abuse are limited because they presume that abuse can be accounted for by the operation of a single-factor cause (e.g., a parent's psychopathology or a family's socioeconomic disadvantage). In contrast, it is possible to conceptualize the development of child-abusive behavior in a more complex manner which takes into account social–psychological (Burgess & Conger, 1978), learning history (Crozier & Katz, 1979; Dubanowski, Evans, & Higuchi, 1978), and parent skill (Wolfe, Kaufman, Aragona, & Sandler, 1981a) variables. Let us now turn our attention in detail to this social-learning formulation of child abuse.

3.2. CHILD ABUSE AS AN EXTREME FORM OF PARENTING

Traditional descriptions of child-abusive parents, heavily influenced by psychopathology and medical model assumptions, often created the impression that these are people who are somehow different, fundamentally and qualitatively, than other parents. However, rather than viewing child abuse as a qualitatively discrete disorder, it is possible to conceptualize physically abusive behavior as one endpoint of an entire range of parenting strategies. For example, if we were to survey the conduct of parents, we would expect to find some who are never physically punitive toward their children, who rarely spank for misbehavior, and who exclusively utilize positive child-control strategies. This group of parents constitutes one end of a child-management range. Much more common, however, are those parents who occasionally use physical discipline to handle certain child misbehavior; they would fall within the large central portion of the child-management spectrum. At the other extreme are parents who rely heavily on physical punishment as a primary method to control their children's behavior. As a result of the frequency or intensity of punitive management style toward their children, some of these parents do injure their youngsters and, consequently, can become designated as abusive.

Construing violence in parenting style along a continuum, with an extremely nonviolent repertoire at one pole and an extremely punitive repertoire at the other, is actually an oversimplification. How a parent chooses to discipline a child, like most other social behavior, is likely to be determined by a number of situational factors (Mischel, 1968), including the specific misbehavior of the child, the parent's perception of the *intent* of the child's action (e.g., whether the child is seen as throwing a tantrum to "make the parent" angry), the parent's own frustration level, or the location where the incident takes place. Nonetheless, abusive parents can be seen as those who are likely to respond to their children in an overly punitive manner, a pattern consistent with evidence that they have difficulty controlling child misbehavior nonviolently (Mastria *et al.*, 1979; Wolfe & Sandler, 1981; Wolfe *et al.*, 1982) and handle even routine interactions with their children more negatively than most parents (Burgess & Conger, 1977b, & 1978).

The central point here is that one can think of child abuse, not as a qualitatively distinctive psychopathological disorder, but instead as the consequence of a parent's overly harsh, violent approach to child management. If parents differ in their reliance on physically punitive controls, they will also differ in their potential for causing injury to a child in the course of discipline. Of both conceptual and applied importance are the issues of how parents develop potentially abusive child-management styles, what factors maintain these styles, and how this form of extreme parenting can be altered.

3.3. THE SOCIAL LEARNING OF ABUSIVE PARENTING

From a social-learning perspective, one can account for an individual's actions by examining that person's own prior learning history, as well as by identifying current factors that operate to maintain or change behavior. In the case of child abuse, it is reasonable to focus particular attention on the principles by which parents learn their child-management style and their manner of coping with anger and frustration. Understanding the principles of behavior development and maintenance in these areas can also help us understand the conduct of abusive parents.

3.3.1. Observational Learning of Punitive Child-Management Techniques

Modeling, or the process of acquiring skills through the observation of others, is a major social-learning principle that explains the development of a wide variety of prosocial and deviant behaviors (Bandura & Walters, 1963). Because the primary, personal models for learning how to parent are usually one's *own* parents, it is not surprising that investigators have found at least moderate communality between the child-management style currently practiced by parents and the behavior that had been modeled by their own parents (Bandura & Walters, 1963).

As we discussed in the preceding chapter, abusive individuals frequently report they had parents who treated them harshly when they were young. If a major source of learning is through observational experiences in one's own family, and if the abusers' reports of their own maltreatment are correct, these are individuals who apparently had a history of exposure to violent styles of parenting and limited exposure to parent models for appropriate, nonviolent child-management techniques. Consequently, physically abusive styles can be seen as a product, in part, of one's own observational learning history.

It is well-established that people acquire complex social behaviors as a result of observational learning. Research also suggests that exposure to modeled aggression increases one's personal tolerance of violence (Berkowitz, 1962; Felsenthal, 1976; Lovaas, 1961). Due to past exposure to intrafamily violence, an individual would not only observe models for this type of parenting style, but would also develop an attitudinal tolerance or acceptance of highly punitive behavior toward children.

3.3.2. Isolation from Sources of Appropriate Information on Parenting

While observational learning based on early experiences in one's own family is a factor that can influence the development of abusive parenting styles, it is clear that exposure to violent parenting models alone is probably insufficient to produce abusive behavior. Even if an individual is raised in a violent family environment, there are presumably many other sources later in life that can provide corrective, re-educational information on more appropriate ways to handle children. Friends, neighbors, family members, one's spouse, and other social supports are all potential sources of everyday information on how to parent.

However, current data on child-abusive parents suggest that they may have less practical access to these information sources than other parents. For example, if abusive parents are socially isolated (Green, 1976; Holmes *et al.*, 1975; Parke & Collmer, 1975; Spinetta, 1978), they will have fewer close friends and neighbors to whom they can turn for everyday child rearing advice. If the abusive parent is a single parent or is experiencing severe marital discord (Bennie & Sclare, 1969; Ebbin *et al.*, 1969; Ory & Earp, 1980; Young, 1964), opportunities to collaborate with one's spouse on the development of appropriate child-management techniques are reduced. Finally, if a currently abusive parent was raised by abusive parents, his or her own parental family would not be a likely source of information on more appropriate ways to handle children. Thus, these seem to be individuals having few people in their environment with whom they are close and to whom they can turn for useful information about raising children.

3.3.3. Children Who Are Difficult to Manage

As we saw in Chapter 2, a number of investigations have shown that some abused children exhibit characteristics that could make them difficult to manage effectively, such as "hyperactivity," noncompliance, irritability, and lower intellectual level (Baldwin & Oliver, 1975; Friedrich & Boriskin, 1976; Milow & Lourie, 1964). If such children are "matched" with parents having a limited repertoire of effective child-management skills, the likelihood of parental frustration and escalating punitiveness would increase.

It is important to note that children who are the targets of parental violence do not always exhibit severe behavior problems or intellectual/developmental impairment, and that a child's actions which elicit abuse may be behaviors entirely normal among children of the abused child's age (Friedman *et al.*, 1981; Scott, 1973; Weston, 1968). This can be accounted for in several ways. For parents who do not understand what to expect from a child, even such routine behaviors as a two-year-old's crying, a three-year-old's bedwetting, or a four-year-old's occasional tantrumming may be *seen* as extraordinary problems when they really are not. A parent lacking knowledge of normal child behavior can label and define as problematic various child actions that more knowledgeable parents realize are normal. Alternatively, and as we will discuss fully later in this chapter, various stressors present in the parent's life can function to reduce her or his adaptability and frustration tolerance, so the parent overreacts even to relatively minor annoyances caused by the child.

3.3.4. The Development and Escalation of Punitive Controls over Child Behavior

To this point, it has been suggested that many abusive parents lack an effective repertoire of skills to handle their children's behavior. The abused child may, in fact, present behavior problems of some kind, or the parent may incorrectly perceive the child's normal conduct as problematic. In either event, at some point the parent begins to respond to the youngster using violent, punishment-oriented techniques.

To understand how relatively common parental punishment practices such as occasional spanking can escalate into high-frequency, high-intensity violence within certain families, we should first consider several characteristics of punishment:

Physical punishment can, in fact, be effective for controlling a child's behavior. Most parents are aware that punishment can be used to control or discipline a child's misbehavior, and most parents report that they use such punishments as spanking on at least an occasional basis (Gelles, 1978). Presumably, abusive parents differ from their nonabusive counterparts because they punish their children more frequently and/or with greater intensity of punishment. However, the practice of responding to a child's misbehavior by physical force is probably maintained by these parents because it does work, at least temporarily; abusive parents may find that they can suppress their children's aversive actions by spanking or hitting the youngster. Especially if a parent lacks the knowledge or skill repertoire to handle problem situations with a child nonviolently (Crozier & Katz, 1979; Doctor & Singer, 1978; Friedman *et al.*, 1981; Wolfe *et al.*, 1981a), punitive control efforts will occur.

Because children appear to "acclimate" to punishment, the parent who relies on punitive controls must over time escalate the intensity of punishment to maintain its effectiveness. A number of studies suggest that organisms adapt to intensities of punishment (Azrin, 1958; Azrin, Holz, & Hake, 1963; Reynolds, 1975). Initially, a relatively low level of punishment (like that of a single light spank) might be sufficiently aversive to suppress a child's behavior. However, if a parent spanks frequently, the child can acclimate to the initial intensity of punishment, thereby requiring the parent to respond in a more intensely aversive manner to achieve the same effect. As the child then adapts to this new level, even more severe punishment may be needed. In this way, we can conceptualize an escalation of punitive responses as the parent attempts to control his or her child's behavior through this mode of discipline. As punishment intensifies, the risk of physical injury to the child also increases.

Physical punishment results in less permanent behavior suppression than do other forms of discipline. While a parent's use of physical punishment can result in the reduction of a child's misbehavior, reliance on this form of aversive control tends to produce temporary behavior suppression rather than enduring change (see Aronfreed, 1968, for an excellent discussion of this issue). Since abusive parents interact with their children in a more punitive, negative manner than nonabusive parents (Burgess & Conger, 1978), they may therefore encounter frequent recurrences of problem situations in everyday child management.

To summarize this aspect of our social-learning analysis of child abuse, it is possible to view many abusive parents as deficient in those skills that are needed to interact effectively with their children. Potential reasons for this deficit include the parent's observational learning of a violent management style from his or her own parents, an attitudinal acceptance of physical punitiveness as a means to handle children's misbehavior, and isolation from potential sources of corrective information on appropriate child-management techniques. If a parent has a limited and largely punitive repertoire of child-management responses, it is likely that he or she will encounter repeated difficulties controlling the child's behavior and may progressively escalate the force and/or the frequency of discipline. As this process of ineffective but frequent physical discipline continues, the child will be at increasing risk to suffer injury.

3.4. ANGER-CONTROL AND COPING-SKILL DEFICITS OF ABUSIVE PARENTS

There is widespread evidence suggesting that abusive parents are often under stress, and that their inability to cope effectively with life frustrations also increases the likelihood of violence directed toward their children. Stressful arousal during difficult parent–child interactions (Disbrow *et al.*, 1977; Frodi & Lamb, 1980; Wolfe *et al.*, in press); frustration as a result of economic, interpersonal, and financial problems (Bennie & Sclare, 1969; Gaines *et al.*, 1978; Gelles, 1973; Gil, 1975; Young, 1964); and anger-control difficulties (Green, 1976; Helfer *et al.*, 1977; Kempe *et al.*, 1962; Steele & Pollock, 1968) have all been cited as problem areas that can increase the potential for abusive episodes to occur. Unfortunately, few investigations have described specifically how life stressors such as these actually trigger episodes of child-abusive behavior. However, more general theories of stress and aggression can provide at least some tentative explanations for the occurrence of such violence in families.

3.4.1. Frustration–Aggression Theory

One of the earliest general theories of aggressive behavior is what has been termed the "frustration–aggression" hypothesis (Dollard, Doob, Miller, Mowrer, & Sears, 1939). According to this model, when an individual's goal-directed behavior is blocked, there is an increase in general frustration level and, in turn, an increased likelihood of aggressive behavior of some type. The probability or intensity of aggression is directly related to the degree of frustration being experienced, and the target of aggression may be either the frustrating agent or some other object. When applied to child-abusive families, this formulation leads to the notion that almost any frustrator of the parent's goal-directed behavior (including financial, relationship, or other stress-inducing obstacles) could be capable of producing aggression, perhaps directed toward children.

The proposal of a direct, simple causal relationship between frustration and aggressive behavior has intuitive appeal and does appear to account for at least some instances of violent conduct. However, recent formulations have focused on the more complex interplay of cognitive, physiological, and behavior components of stress and anger.

3.4.2. Cognitive–Behavioral Formulations of Anger

It is possible to construe anger as the result of three influences: *external events, internal or cognitive (thought) processes,* and *behavioral reactions* (Lazarus, 1966; Novaco, 1976, 1978). As described by Novaco (1978), external events include frustrations, annoyances, or other aversive situations in the environment. When confronted with such events, an individual cognitively appraises or interprets them; if the appraisal results in the labeling of one's state as "angry," an aggressive response can be produced. Novaco (1978) stresses the interplay and reciprocal influence of external events, cognitive processes, and behavioral reactions; aggression can be seen not as the direct result of stress, but instead as a result of maladaptive responses to stress.

Extending this formulation to child-abusive acts, we might hypothesize that certain life events (such as losing a job, fighting with one's spouse, or having massive child-care responsibilities) can lead to cognitions of anger, frustration, or loss of control as well as heightened physiological arousal. Depending on the parent's learning history and anger-coping skills, verbal or physical aggression may then occur.

Why, however, should a *child* be the target of this aggression? Several theorists have suggested that once an individual is in a state of elevated arousal that he or she has labeled as "anger," aversive cues in the environment will be likely to elicit aggression (Bandura, 1973; Berkowitz, 1974; Rule & Nesdale, 1976; Wolfe *et al.*, in press). Presumably, a child's crying, an act of noncompliance, or some other misbehavior can serve as an aversive cue that elicits aggression from the parent who is already angry and aroused. Thus, the parent who is angry directs aggression toward a youngster emitting some action the parent finds aversive or unpleasant. Presumably, the same child behavior might *not* elicit such violence if the parent were not already in a heightened state of anger arousal.

This analysis can account for an increased risk of child-abusive behavior among certain parents who are stressed by various life frustrations outside the parent–child relationship. However, another potential source of stress is a parent's own unsuccessful interactions with his or her child. When asked to describe what occurs immediately before a child-abusive episode, some parents report escalating feelings of anger, frustration, and arousal as they try, repeatedly and unsuccessfully, to keep their children from crying, tantrumming, or otherwise misbehaving (cf. Wolfe *et al.*, in press). In these instances, the frustrating event is the child's behavior, which the parent is unable to control effectively. If the parent labels his or her own arousal in the situation as anger, there is an increased likelihood that aggression will be directed toward the child who is emitting aversive cues (such as crying or screaming). If a violent response by the parent *does* successfully terminate the child's aversive behavior, the parent's use of aggressive controls will be reinforced.

From this cognitive–behavioral perspective, aggression is not an inevitable consequence of frustration or emotional arousal, and individuals can learn to develop coping strategies to reduce the probability of violence during difficult situations. One strategy is developing the competencies to alter emotional arousal itself. Identifying cues which signify that one is becoming angry, practicing physical self-relaxation at those times, and utilizing cognitive self-calming statements can help an individual maintain control and reduce the likelihood of aggressive responses produced or mediated by anger (Novaco, 1976, 1978). By adopting these strategies, the parent is essentially learning to remain calm and unaroused in situations that previously elicited aggression.

Control of anger arousal in difficult situations is only one part of an effective coping strategy. The second component is developing those behavioral competencies needed to handle the frustrating situation successfully. Teaching a person merely to relax while a child repeatedly tantrums or to remain calm whenever one feels overwhelmed due to living problems such as joblessness or difficulties in social relationships is not likely to produce enduring change. Instead, competencies for handling or changing the frustrating, anger-inducing events are needed. Thus, the mother who becomes angry when she is unable to control her child's behavior may need to acquire not only anger-control skills, but also specific skills of child management. An individual who becomes enraged when others take advantage of him may need not only to control his temper, but also to develop the assertion skills to deal more effectively with the unreasonable actions of others. And, frustrations due to unemployment may call for specific assistance in job finding. To the extent that instances of aggression toward a child are functionally related to the parent's inability to deal effectively with anger or frustration, the acquisition of coping skills to handle these problems is necessary.

3.5. IMPLICATIONS FOR TREATMENT

As we are conceptualizing it, child-abusive behavior can often be seen as the consequence of certain skill deficits of parents. Based upon the research literature on child-abusive families, as well as a social-learning model of how violence occurs, three major areas can be identified as potentially problematic for abusive individuals. These are deficits in *child-management skills*, deficits in *anger-control skills*, and the presence of *life-style risk factors* that can impair a family's overall functioning.

3.5.1. Child-Management Skill Deficits as Contributors to Abuse

As we discussed earlier, parents who rely on excessive, physically punitive methods to handle child misbehavior can become caught in a cycle in which they use increasingly intense and frequent punishment to manage their children. The bulk of data now available on abusive parents' child-management styles suggests that (1) these individuals have had limited personal exposure to nonviolent methods of child management, (2) their use of punitive behavior is maintained because it results in at least temporary suppression of the child's aversive behavior, and (3) the abused child may exhibit aversive actions or behavior problems that call for management skills which the parent lacks. As a parent responds to aversive child behavior with increasingly frequent or increasingly intense forms of punishment, the risk of injury to the child also becomes higher. Patterson (1976) has termed this a "coercive" family cycle, in which both the parents and the child engage in escalating rates of aversive behavior toward one another.

Intervention for this pattern requires training parents to use more appropriate, effective, and nonviolent child-management techniques. Parents can be taught methods for controlling their children's difficult misbehaviors without physical violence and thereby reduce the likelihood of injury during disciplinary episodes. Concurrently, training in the use of positive reinforcement techniques with children broadens the parent's repertoire of management skills and permits the establishment of a more rewarding relationship between them. The aims of child-management skills training, then, are to reduce the parent's reliance on inappropriately aversive controls and increase the use of positive methods of behavior management.

3.5.2. Anger-Control Deficits as Contributors to Abuse

It is axiomatic that violent, aggressive responses are more likely to occur when an individual is in a state of heightened anger than when the person is calm and unaroused. Clinical reports of child abuse frequently describe these parents as being angry at the time of the violent incident,and the types of traumatic injuries sustained by abused children are generally more consistent with violence occurring when the parent is angered than with the infliction of harm in a calm, intentional, premeditated fashion (Smith & Hanson, 1974). If parents can be taught to cope with anger more effectively, the likelihood of aggressive responses should be reduced.

One set of stimuli capable of eliciting anger is aversive behavior of the child. Anger when a child cries, tantrums, or exhibits noncompliant behavior with the parent may elicit angry arousal and serve as a cue which facilitates aggression toward the youngster. This would appear especially likely if the parent has an unsuccessful history of calmly handling these aversive actions and is more frustrated by them. In these cases, training in anger-control skills is focused directly on difficult interactions between the parent and the child.

As we discussed earlier, frustrating events occurring outside the parent–child interaction can also induce anger. Difficulties in interpersonal relationships, economic stressors, and a wide range of other problems may produce a heightened level of arousal labeled by the individual as anger. At such times, aversive behavior by the child can result in aggressive responses toward him or her. Consequently, anger-control intervention may need to be focused, in at least some cases, on events outside the parent–child interaction itself.

3.5.3. Life-Style Risk Factors as Contributors to Abuse

Certain life-style conditions and problems appear to affect adversely the functioning of families. As we discussed earlier, the presence of overwhelming child care responsibilities, social isolation of the parent, socioeconomic stress, and marital discord have all been linked to an increased incidence of child abuse. Presumably, these forms of external stress serve to increase the general frustration level of parents and lead them to feel overwhelmed and isolated from sources of reinforcement. As Gil (1975) points out, variables such as socioeconomic stress and isolation from community resources can best be viewed as "context" factors that increase the likelihood of a variety of problems in some families. One of those problems is child-directed violence.

If joblessness, social isolation, excessive child care responsibilities, or poor everyday problem-solving skills impair the adaptive functioning of an abusive family, they also require treatment attention. As we will see, intervention for such problems may involve arranging for the family to receive some social support service to meet that need (e.g., the parents obtaining welfare benefits, placing the child in a low-cost day care center). In other cases, specific types of skills training (such as job-finding skill, social skill, or problem-solving skill training) may be required to help the parent cope more effectively with frustration and living difficulties.

Thus, the treatment of child-abusive families is directed toward enhancing the child management and anger/frustration coping repertoire of the parent, together with reducing any life-style risk factors associated with abuse. Since multiple factors are often responsible for abusive behavior (Belsky, 1978; Burgess, 1979; Dubanowski *et al.*, 1978), a family may require several different forms of treatment during the course of their intervention (such as child-management training combined with instruction in anger control). Determining the treatment needs of a family first requires a careful assessment of the circumstances which led to previous instances of child maltreatment. Therefore, we will now turn our attention to techniques for family assessment.

4

The Clinical Assessment of Child-Abusive Families

In previous chapters, we considered a number of different characteristics and parent skill deficits that appear capable of producing child-abusive behavior. It should be evident, however, that an important clinical task is determining *which* specific factors are responsible for the abusive actions in a *given* family. For example, child-management deficits, lack of knowledge about children, anger-control problems, joblessness or socioeconomic stress, and child-developmental handicaps have all been found to occur disproportionately more often among abusive families. (However, these factors are based on group "mean differences" and they do not tell a clinician what variable, or set of variables, are the antecedents of abusive conduct for a given family seeking treatment.) The first task of a therapist intervening with an abusive family is to determine carefully the critical factors which lead to child maltreatment in that particular family.

In this chapter, we will first discuss several special matters affecting the initial assessment of child-abusive families. Then, problem areas that merit close assessment attention will be identified and described. Finally, specific procedures and techniques for evaluating each of these problem areas will be considered.

4.1. SPECIAL ISSUES IN THE ASSESSMENT OF ABUSIVE FAMILIES

There are several ways in which the initial assessment of a child-abusive family differs from the evaluation of most other cases seen in an outpatient treatment setting. These include (1) difficulties associated with the assessment of "socially undesirable" private family behavior, (2) the often mandated, as opposed to voluntary, nature of an abusive family's treatment, and (3) the need for unusually clear definition of the therapist's and the family's mutual responsibilities related to treatment.

4.1.1. The Assessment of Socially Undesirable Private Behavior

As previous investigators have pointed out, an important problem in the evaluation of child-abusive families is that the behaviors of primary interest—the parent's actual episodes of maltreatment and violence toward the child—occur privately within the family and are not, for the most part, observable directly by the therapist (Friedman *et al.*, 1981). In many abusive families, violent behavior occurs with relatively low frequency, also making it difficult to observe directly. Further, because abusive conduct is socially undesirable, parents may be less likely to describe accurately their own family violence than they would be to report problems that do not carry such a social stigma.

Because actual abusive conduct cannot be directly observed under most circumstances, both assessment and treatment attention must be focused on antecedents which are functionally related to the actual maltreatment. For example, if a mother strikes her child because she is unable to stop the child's extended tantrums using less extreme means, a possible antecedent to the violent behavior involves the parent's lack of child-management skills. If another parent exhibits unreasonable harsh punishment toward his child only on days when he is frustrated and angry following problems at work, antecedent variables of importance might include the parent's anger-control and problem-solving skills. Because abusive behavior can rarely be directly observed, it is necessary to focus assessment attention on those circumstances which give rise to violence capable of producing injury to the child. If functionally relevant antecedent conditions can be identified and altered, the likelihood of violent behavior capable of injuring the child can also be reduced.

4.1.2. Mandated versus Voluntary Treatment

As we noted in Chapter 1, parents become labeled or designated as "abusive" following social welfare–judicial proceedings that are primarily concerned with protecting the child's well-being. These same proceedings are usually responsible for the abusive family's presence in treatment. In contrast to the manner in which most families seek out voluntary treatment for difficulties that they themselves consider to be problematic, abusive families often enter treatment because they are required to. Depending on the case, parents might be told they must receive therapy to regain custody of their child, to have their child returned home, or as a step toward terminating the child-protective service's involvement in their affairs. A parent may or may not actually *believe* that his or her conduct toward the child is a problem that requires treatment.

Therapy of any form, when it is externally mandated rather than voluntarily requested, presents special problems of client compliance, motivation, and candor when reporting behavior change. For this reason, it is important to clarify with parents, even before any formal assessment begins, the purpose and nature of the therapist's contact with them.

4.1.3. Clear Definition of Therapist and Family Responsibilities

When abusive families are first seen in treatment, there has usually been an investigation by social welfare authorities of the alleged abuse incident, often accompanied by formal court hearings to evaluate the child's well-being. At this point, parents are often antagonistic and hostile toward child welfare agency staff, the court that ordered or recommended family treatment, and the therapist who will be providing treatment. From the parents' perspective, all of this external, evaluative involvement in their family affairs is probably seen as an unwanted intrusion that questions the parents' values, skill, and concern for their children. In point of fact, the welfare agency investigation process often *does* question just these things. However, by the time treatment of a family is requested, the case investigation aspect of determining whether a parent behaved abusively has presumably ended. At this point, the establishment of a constructive, problem-solving, and nonaccusatory therapy relationship becomes critical. Several factors can aid in this process.

4.1.3.1. Avoiding the Use of Accusatory Language and Behavior Descriptions

In our clinic, parents are never asked to "confess" to being abusive and the term "abusive" is itself very rarely used. Because of the exceedingly negative and accusatory connotation of this label, parents may react defensively to therapists who use it with them. Instead, an initial assessment session might begin with the therapist explaining that he or she understands the parent has had problems managing the child effectively, that the child is difficult to handle, that the parent has been experiencing problems with temper, or so on depending on information already known by the therapist. While one never seeks to minimize the seriousness of child maltreatment episodes, excessively judgmental or accusatory comments by the therapist are likely to elicit little useful information (and, conceivably, a good deal of defensiveness) by the parent who feels accused.

4.1.3.2. Defining Therapy in a Problem-Solving Manner

While the exact plan and content of a therapy intervention cannot be described until the family has been fully assessed, abusive parents may not understand what treatment is for or how they might benefit from it. Prior to detailed assessment, the therapist should outline a general plan for intervention in a way that the parent can grasp. This outline can begin by explaining the therapist's intention to gather information about the child and his/her behavior problems, the parent's current disciplinary practices, and the presence of difficulties in the parent's life that are frustrating. The parent should then be given a general description of the types of treatment that might be used, such as assistance in learning to handle the child's misbehavior differently, learning to handle anger more effectively, or dealing better with life frustrations. If this information is conveyed initially, the parent is more likely to grasp the nature of treatment as a problem-solving, skills-training, and educationally based endeavor.

4.1.3.3. Clarifying the Relationship between the Therapist and Child Welfare Authorities

If the therapist seeing the family is someone other than the family's caseworker, it is important to explain the relationship that exists between the therapist and child-protective or court authorities. For example, parents might be told that as part of the welfare department's plan, they are being asked to attend sessions at the mental health center, family counseling center, or whatever agency is providing treatment. It is also useful to explain how and when the therapist plans to communicate with authorities concerning the family's attendance and progress. As we will discuss in detail later in this chapter, the development of an objective and behaviorally oriented treatment contract is often a useful way to clarify how the therapist will report progress to child welfare authorities, the court, or others who are legally mandated with overall responsibility for the child's well-being.

4.2. A MODEL FOR FAMILY ASSESSMENT

The purpose of assessment in cases of child abuse is to determine what specific factors in the family appear to be responsible for maltreatment of the child. As we discussed earlier, it is important for a clinician to recognize that not all instances of excessive violence directed toward children result in physical injury that is detected (or detectable) by others. Therefore, rather than examining only those episodes that have resulted in a known physical injury to a child, it is more critical to focus assessment attention on those factors which produce excessive parental violence, regardless of whether all instances of that violence cause injury to the child. As an example, if a parent beats a child 10 times over a 6-month period but causes a serious physical injury on only one of those occasions, assessment attention would *not* focus only on the single instance that produced an injury. Instead, we would seek to assess and alter the parent's pattern of beating the child, since this is the unacceptably violent behavior capable of producing injury to the youngster. Assessment, then, is directed at identifying antecedents of the family's violence toward the child, not just those specific episodes of violence resulting in an injury which someone (such as a physician, teacher, caseworker, or nurse) has detected.

4.2.1. Key Areas for Attention in Family Assessment

Based on our earlier review of the child abuse literature and on a social-learning model of family violence, it is possible to identify a number of areas that should receive close attention by the therapist who is initially evaluating an abusive family. Table 2 lists and briefly describes some of these critical assessment areas.

The major tasks of a clinician are to evaluate whether problems such as those listed in Table 2 affect the abusive family and to then make a preliminary judgment about whether the identified difficulties are causally related to episodes of parental violence. The matter of judging "causality" in clinical treatment cases is frequently difficult;

TABLE 2
Areas That Should Receive Attention When Evaluating Child-Abusive Families

Area or problem	Assessment questions in relation to abuse
Severe parental psychopathology (psychosis, sociopathy, substance abuse)	Does the parent exhibit a psychotic disorder responsible for the episodes of abusive behavior? Does the parent seek to intentionally harm the child in a sociopathic manner? Are

(*continued*)

TABLE 2 (*Continued*)

Area or problem	Assessment questions in relation to abuse
	episodes of violence correlated with parental substance abuse, such as alcohol or drug intoxication?
Child-management deficits and child behavior control problems	Is abusive conduct the result of the parent's inability to control child misbehavior using appropriate, nonviolent management techniques? Does the parent lack those management skills needed to handle the child's problem behaviors?
Parent/child interaction skill deficits	Apart from discrete "critical" management problems described above, is the parent able to interact effectively with the child in everyday situations (such as talking with the child, playing, or giving commands)?
Insufficient knowledge about child development and behavior	Does the parent have unreasonably high expectations for the child's behavior given the youngster's age and level of development? Do these unreasonable expectations lead to frustration and difficulties with the child?
Anger-control deficits	Do abuse episodes occur when the parent becomes angry and upset, and because the parent lacks the skills to handle anger without violence?
Family stressors and problem-solving skills inadequate to deal with those stressors	Is the occurrence of abuse associated with identifiable life stressors or frustrations, such as economic difficulties, joblessness, interpersonal frustrations of family members, or similar factors? Are the parents coping effectively with life stressors?
Social isolation	Does the parent have an adequate social support network to meet his/her own needs and to provide social gratification? Are there people to whom the parent can turn for reasonable advice on child-management matters?

determining what *causes* a particular parent's child-abusive behavior is even more problematic given the importance of providing treatment to abusive families as quickly as possible, and not placing a child at risk while the therapist studies causes of the parent's abusive conduct. For these reasons, clinicians may be ethically limited to making assumptions about the causes of a parent's violent behavior, and later assessing the apparent validity of those assumptions through evidence of reduction in the parent's violence when the problem has been treated.

As an example, a clinician might believe that the antecedent factors responsible for one mother's abusive conduct are (1) a lack of effective management skills for handling her child's misbehavior nonviolently and (2) difficulties in anger control and stressful overarousal during episodes of child misbehavior. The information that leads the therapist to this formulation may include assessment findings that physical violence toward the child always occurs when the child is misbehaving (throwing tantrums or crying), the parent has little knowledge of ways to control effectively child misbehavior other than by spanking, and the parent reports feeling angry and "out of control" when difficult problems occur with her child. Based on this information, and assuming that other causal factors are not also operating, a reasonable intervention plan is to teach the parent more effective child-management strategies and to help her acquire anger-control skills. At a point following intervention, the therapist would hope to find that episodes of severe spanking and anger have decreased or been eliminated. While such case improvement cannot "prove" conclusively that the therapist's causal formulation was correct, it is at least *consistent* with the initial clinical hypothesis regarding the cause of the parent's abusive actions. In the applied treatment of child-abusive families, an intervention can be considered clinically relevant when it targets for change those problems and skill deficits that are functionally related to the family's past history of violence.

4.2.2. Format and Duration of Initial Family Evaluation

Preintervention assessment of an abusive family begins with the therapist's first contact with the family and ends when the therapist has developed relatively specific assumptions or hypotheses concerning the causes of the family's abusive behavior. Depending on the complexity of the case, this process may require a number of assessment sessions and the therapist may be called upon to use a variety of different assessment techniques. We will discuss using these techniques in detail as we turn our attention to evaluating potential problem areas in the abusive family, but some of the major assessment procedures available to the therapist include:

- *Detailed interviews with the parent* to obtain the parent's report about family problems and stressors, the child's behavior and disciplinary practices currently used, and circumstances surrounding previous episodes of harsh treatment of the youngster.
- *Information obtained from child welfare caseworkers* including the caseworker's evaluation of past family problems and observations regarding the family's present functioning and social needs.
- *Structured inventories and questionnaires* that assess the parent's knowledge of child development, behavior problems of the child, and anger-control difficulties and can supplement information obtained by interviews alone, at least for those parents who are able to complete self-report measures.
- *Parent self-monitoring of critical events that occur at home* such as instances of child misbehavior, situations when the parent felt it necessary to spank the child, times when the parent felt stressed or out-of-control, and so on depending on the information sought by the therapist.
- *Direct behavioral observation of parent–child interactions,* at home or in the clinic, to obtain information on the child's behavior and the parents' strategies for dealing with the youngster's behavior.

The use of multiple assessment techniques is desirable when evaluating most clinical problems, and it is especially helpful when assessing the child-abusive family. By relying on a combination of measures (interview–verbal self-report, direct observation, inventory-based, self-monitoring, and agency record data), it is possible to obtain a comprehensive and specific picture of the functioning of the abusive family.

We will now turn our attention to using these techniques to assess some of the key problem areas that may be responsible for a family's violent behavior.

4.3. ASSESSMENT OF PARENT PSYCHOPATHOLOGY

While demonstrable parent psychopathology does not account for most instances of child abuse (Friedman *et al.*, 1981; Kempe, 1973; Kempe & Kempe, 1978), the consistent finding that a small minority of abusive parents can be diagnosed as severely disturbed suggests that a therapist should rule out the presence of severe psychopathology before beginning intervention. Two forms of psychopathology most critical to rule out are parental psychosis and sociopathic disorders. The parent who inflicts injury on a child while grossly psychotic or the parent who sociopathically and intentionally plans to harm a youngster can be seen as individuals who require treatment for their own individual disturbances. For example, if a parent is psychotically delusional, disoriented, or hallucinating during episodes of abuse, an appropriate initial target for intervention is the psychotic disorder. Similarly, if a parent derives gratification from planning sociopathic ways to injure a child intentionally, a fundamental change in this behavioral disposition must occur before further intervention can be effective. Given this relative lack of success in altering other sociopathic behavior of adults (Newcomer, 1980), treating abusive parents of this type may be exceedingly difficult. Fortunately, the current research literature indicates that sociopathically abusive parents are quite rare.

The primary methods to assess the presence of severe psychopathology are by observing the parent's behavior during interviews and obtaining historical information from both the parent and other sources (such as family members or social service agency records). Evidence of psychotic perceptual and cognitive distortions, or indications that the parent derives gratification (and feels no remorse or anxiety) from intentionally injuring the child, each suggest that the possible role of severe psychopathology be explored. While empirical data do not exist concerning the types of abusive acts afflicted by severely disturbed parents, the presence of bizarre, premeditated, or ritualistically inflicted child injuries should always lead the therapist to evaluate closely the parent's own emotional functioning.

4.3.1. Child Abuse Episodes Correlated with Parent Substance Abuse

Several investigators have noted that certain parents behave abusively (or behave more abusively) when they are under the influence of alcohol intoxicants or other chemical substances (Blumberg, 1974; Johnson & Morse, 1968; Young, 1964). While current research does not indicate that substance abuse is a causal factor in most cases of child abuse, there are undoubtedly some parents whose behavior becomes more aggressive, uninhibited, and less frustration-tolerant during periods of substance abuse. In these instances, the effects of the intoxicating substance can function as a controlling or discriminative variable which increases the likelihood of the parent's violent behavior while the parent is intoxicated.

It is somewhat inappropriate to classify substance abuse patterns as a form of parent "psychopathology." However, the two can be conceptualized similarly in relation to abusive behavior: in each case, aggressive behavior can be more likely to occur due to the effects of an "intraparent" factor, whether that factor is the parent's psychotic thinking or substance intoxication. Consequently, one aspect of intervention is to target the relevant controlling variable. Should interviews with the parent or data obtained from other sources (family members, social welfare records, or so on) indicate that episodes of past violence are associated with periods of substance intoxication, a logical part of treatment is intervening to reduce the chemical abuse pattern.

4.4. ASSESSMENT OF CHILD-MANAGEMENT DEFICITS AND CHILD BEHAVIOR CONTROL PROBLEMS

If abusive behavior directly traceable to parent psychopathology factors appears to be relatively uncommon, the role of child-management skill deficits is receiving much closer attention in the child abuse literature. As we discussed in detail earlier, the rationale for this attention is that extreme violence toward a child can result from the parent's inability to handle problem situations in an effective, nonviolent manner. To the clinician evaluating an abusive family, assessment of child-management problems should address a series of related questions:

1. Does inappropriate, violent parent behavior follow periods of child misbehavior? Is the parent using excessive force to control the youngster's misbehavior?
2. What specific child misbehaviors elicit parental violence?
3. How, exactly, is the parent now handling the child in these "critical" problem situations (e.g., yelling, spanking, hitting the child with an object)?
4. What is the frequency and topography of child-management problem situations (e.g., how often do these problems occur, what time of day do they occur, what events precede the child's misbehavior)?
5. What nonviolent management skills *should* the parent be using to control the child's behavior in these situations?

The therapist assessing this aspect of a family's functioning seeks to determine whether the parent is behaving abusively in certain situations because he or she is unable to control the child without using excessive physical force. There are several techniques that can be used to evaluate child-management skill deficits. These include (1) interviews with the parent, (2) inventories to assess child behavior problems (3) self-monitoring of problem situations, and (4) direct observation of parent–child interactions.

4.4.1. Interviewing to Assess Possible Child-Management Problems

A useful way to obtain initial information concerning child-management skill deficits is by discussing, with the parent, whether the child exhibits behavior problems and how the parent currently disciplines the youngster. This discussion can focus both on situations where the parent is known to have behaved violently toward the child (e.g., the specific episodes which led to the parent being considered abusive), as well as other day-to-day difficulties the parent encounters with the child.

As we noted earlier, it is important to avoid giving abusive parents the feeling that the therapist's purpose is to determine whether they are "bad" or "inept" parents. If this impression is conveyed, the parent may become reluctant to provide accurate information about the child's behavior and his or her own current disciplinary practices. Instead, it is reassuring for parents to learn that *all* children are difficult to handle at times, and that the therapist's aim is to get an accurate picture of the child's behavior problems and the parent's current discipline so the therapist can provide advice on more effective ways to handle the child. When approached in this way, parents feel less defensive and become more actively, cooperatively involved in the problem-solving nature of treatment.

The exact conduct of this type of interview will vary from therapist to therapist, but the aim is to "identify" situations with the child that the parent finds difficult, or which require excessive force for the parent to handle. It is particularly useful for the therapist to assess not only child-management problem situations, but also the *antecedents* of those situations (what leads up to them) and the current *consequences* (how the parent now handles the problem or what happens when the child behaves in this way).

As one example of this interview strategy, we might consider a clinical case study reported by Wolfe, Kelly, and Drabman (1981). In this report, a mother was referred to treatment by welfare authorities following evidence of bruises and lacerations to her 4- and 9-year-old children. After the therapist had ruled out the presence of severe parent psychopathology, interview attention focused on possible management problems with her children and the circumstances surrounding all previous beating episodes. By inquiring into various difficulties the parent experienced with the youngsters, the therapist was able to pinpoint one clear and recurring problem situation: excessive, noncompliant dawdling in the morning. The antecedents of this problem included the mother's requests that the children get ready to leave the house for school and the children's noncompliance with her requests. As the noncompliant dawdling continued, the parent repeated her requests, but these were generally ignored until the parent "lost her temper." At this point, the children were spanked and, over time, the mother spanked with greater intensity. One of these morning spankings ultimately resulted in injury to one of the children and referral to our clinic.

In this case, interview data were used to pinpoint a child-management problem situation that resulted in excessive, and finally abusive, force. Parameters of the problem situation were defined (e.g., that it occurred in the mornings when the children were requested to get ready for school and when the children repeatedly ignored the parent's requests), and the misbehavior's current consequences (spanking and beating) were similarly identified. Since the occurrence of abusive behavior was closely "tied" to this management problem situation, the assessment provided information on an area that would require treatment attention (teaching the parent how to handle the child's noncompliance and dawdling without resorting to physical punishment).

Careful interviewing to identify child-management problem situations often provides a good deal of information on the child's behavior and the parent's current reported disciplinary practices. Structured inventories can be used to guide further the therapist's questioning.

4.4.2. Child Behavior and Parent Management Inventories

When attempting to conceptualize a family's child-management difficulties, a therapist is actually assessing the child's behavior (or misbehavior), as well as the parent's knowledge and skill in dealing with the child. There are a number of self-report inventories that can be used to gain information about both the child's conduct and the parent's knowledge of appropriate management techniques. We will consider two in detail.

The Eyberg Child Behavior Inventory (Eyberg & Ross, 1978) lists 36 common behavior problems of children and asks the parent to indicate how often each behavior occurs, in addition to whether the parent finds the misbehavior problematic. A copy of the Eyberg inventory is found in Appendix I. Parents can complete the scale themselves as a written self-report inventory, or its items can be read aloud to individuals unable to complete the measure in written form. The Eyberg is not an exhaustive list of all possible child behavior problems, and the therapist should be aware that critical, abuse-triggering child-management incidents may not be among those misbehaviors included in the inventory. Nonetheless, it can provide a structured and reasonably comprehensive "starting point" for evaluating child misbehaviors that the parent is unable to handle without violence.

Knowledge of Behavioral Principles as Applied to Children (KBPAC) (O'Dell, Tarler-Benlolo, & Flynn, 1979) is an inventory, completed by the parent, to assess knowledge of behavioral principles of child management. Appendix II presents the items comprising this measure. The respondent is asked to identify the correct way to handle various problems that are exhibited by children, and responses are scored to determine whether the parent reports correct use of child-management techniques.

A desirable feature of this inventory is that it provides the therapist with an initial assessment of the parent's understanding of behaviorally sound procedures for handling child misbehavior. Because the scale's items tap ways to handle problem situations without requiring the use of sophisticated terminology, it does not merely evaluate the parent's knowledge of behavioral terms. However, the number of problem situations presented to the respondent is necessarily limited, and management problems difficult for the parent to handle may not be among those included in the measure. In addition, scale items assess parent *knowledge,* which may not correspond to the parent's actual *skill* when confronted with child misbehavior.

Scales such as the Eyberg Child Behavior Inventory and the KBPAC can best be utilized as initial information-gathering measures and as vehicles that can facilitate more detailed discussion between the therapist and parent on child problems and the way they are now handled. Such inventories assist the clinician in the task of pinpointing problem situations for the family and can be a useful part of assessment.

4.4.3. Self-Monitoring of Child-Management Problems

Interview and inventories can each provide information about child-management difficulties. Another assessment strategy that yields relatively specific data on both child and parent behavior is having the parent monitor problems that occur at home daily. In our clinic, we often ask parents to keep a daily log in which they record *(1) all occasions of child misbehavior, (2) events or antecedents that led to the misbehavior episode,* and *(3) a brief description of how the incident was handled.* Since many parents have difficulty during a single interview in recounting specific instances of child-management problems over the preceding week, maintaining an accurate log of this kind and bringing the records to sessions provides focused information that can be discussed with the therapist. As with information obtained during interviews, self-monitoring data are used by the therapist to identify, as precisely as possible, the specific areas where training in more effective child-management skills will be needed.

When parents are asked to self-monitor their own behavior and the problem behavior of their children, efforts should always be made to keep the actual record-keeping process simple and straightforward. If a parent is instructed to record behavior in an overly detailed, cumbersome, elaborate manner, the "response cost" of the self-monitoring procedure may be so great that the parent will not perform it accurately. It is more successful to provide parents with simple self-monitoring forms on which they record a limited amount of information (a short description of each problem incident, its antecedents, and the way it was handled) that can be discussed more fully with the therapist in the next session. Since self-monitoring requires a parent's efforts and attention outside the session, it is also important for the therapist to explain fully the kind of information being sought, to explain the process is necessary for effective treatment, and to reinforce the client's efforts to monitor behavior. Finally, while self-monitoring is obviously most useful when the target child or children are living with the parent, families in which the youngster has been temporarily removed from the household can monitor that youngster's behavior during home visits or can monitor the behavior of any nonremoved children still in the home.

4.4.4. Direct Observation of Parent–Child Interactions

All of the strategies for assessing child-management problems considered to this point rely on some form of parent self-report. While this is a widely accepted method of assessment (especially when the forms of self-report are varied to include interviews, inventories, and self-monitoring), parents' descriptions of their own behavior and the reported conduct of their children may not correspond with what really takes place during interactions between them. This does not necessarily suggest that the parent is intentionally providing inaccurate information, but may simply reflect the fact that individuals' self-reports of behavior are sometimes inconsistent with actual conduct (cf. Mischel, 1968). For this reason, directly observing the interactions between abusive parents and their children can provide the therapist with additional information on both the child's behavior and the parent's skill in handling the child.

4.4.4.1. At-Home and In-Clinic Observational Settings

Under the most ideal of circumstances, the therapist would be present in the home of the abusive family for extended periods of time to observe parent and child behavior as it naturally takes place. While it is unlikely the observer would see actual episodes of abusive conduct, instances of child misbehavior and examples of how the parent responds to it could be noted. If similar child misbehavior has elicited parental violence in the past, the observer would be viewing potentially explosive interactions as they naturally occur.

Unfortunately, even when home observations can be made, it is rarely feasible for an observer to spend protracted periods of time with an abusive family. Therefore, *when* the therapist or other person visits the family is quite important. Assessment observations are likely to provide the greatest amount of useful information when the observer is watching potentially problematic situations between the parent and child. For example, if a mother reports that her child's tantrums and screaming are difficult to handle without spanking, an ideal time to observe is when these problems usually take place.

There are two ways to arrange the observation of critical incidents. The first is to make home visits at times when problem situations are most likely to occur naturally. If interview data indicate that the parent has problems with the child in the morning, after school, or at bedtime, observations at such identified times can be scheduled.

A second direct observation method is to arrange for the family to engage in specially constructed tasks that are intended to elicit certain child behaviors and parent skills. In this case, the therapist does not attempt to observe problems that occur naturally, but instead contrives interaction tasks to serve as analogues of potential problem situations. As examples of this assessment approach, Wolfe *et al.* (1982) and Crimmins *et al.* (1982) reported the procedure of scattering many small toys and other objects on the living room floor of a client's home and having the abusive parent ask the child to pick all of them up. During the task, the therapist observed the parent's behavior (including style and appropriateness of command-giving, whether the parent reinforced child command-giving, whether the parent reinforced child compliance, and types of controls used) and the child's behavior (reaction to the parent's commands, noncompliance, and so on). In similar fashion, Burgess and Conger (1978) have described the construction of in-the-home staged, competitive games between parents and children in order to study the interactions between them.

If analogue tasks are used for observational–assessment purposes, they should be relevant to problems the family experiences and should approximate situations that may lead to abusive conduct. Thus, if a problem "theme" during interviews involves the parent's inability to handle appropriately repeated child noncompliance, an interaction task which elicits child noncompliance is most likely to provide useful information. In addition, it is desirable to construct interactions that assess cooperative, positive parent and child behavior. Wolfe *et al.* (1982) and Crimmins *et al.* (1981) also observed abusive parents and their young target children during cooperative tasks (such as coloring and playing table games together) to evaluate the parents' skill when interacting positively. Interestingly, both of these investigations found that the parents rarely made positive, warm, or reinforcing comments, even during what were ostensibly cooperative tasks. Consistent with reports that abusive parents direct fewer positive behaviors to their children than nonabusive parents (Burgess & Conger, 1978; Burgess, 1979), deficient performance in these cooperative assessment interactions also suggested the need to train the parents in techniques for reinforcing positive child behavior (beyond nonviolently managing episodes of misbehavior).

Parent–child interactions can be directly observed in the clinic, as well as in the family's home. In most reports using in-clinic interaction assessments (Crimmins *et al.*, 1982; Mastria *et al.*, 1979; Wolfe *et al.*, 1982), the parent and child are observed as they engage in some extended task in a playroom setting. Performance in tasks designed to elicit child misbehavior (such as having the parent direct the child to pick up and sort play objects) and positive behavior (e.g., the parent and child playing games or playing with toys) can be used for assessment purposes.

4.4.4.2. Rating Parent and Child Behaviors

As the therapist observes parent–child interactions, whether in the home or in the clinic and whether naturally occurring or during a contrived interaction task, it is necessary to develop a system to assess what is taking place. The aim is to identify elements of the parent–child interaction that can be targeted for later child-management skills training.

A number of investigators have developed very detailed and comprehensive systems for coding parent–child interaction behavior. Patterson and his colleagues (Patterson, Ray, Shaw, & Cobb, 1969), for example, developed a procedure for observationally coding interactions on as many as 29 different behaviors. Within the child abuse literature specifically, several skill deficits have been identified among abusive parents and merit the therapist's close attention when observing a family's interactions:

- *Deficient positive verbal comments* to the child, reflecting the parent's failure to attend, recognize, and praise the child's positive or on-task behavior (Burgess & Conger, 1978; Mastria *et al.*, 1979; Sandler *et al.*, 1978; Wolfe *et al.*, 1982).
- *Deficient positive physical behavior*, such as affectionate touching,

to convey approval when the child behaves well (Crimmins *et al.*, 1982; Sandler *et al.*, 1978; Wolfe *et al.*, 1982).

- *Deficient frequency of verbal contacts* with the child, including infrequent appropriately phrased commands and directions and general inattentiveness toward the child (Burgess & Conger, 1977a, 1978; Crimmins *et al.*, 1982).
- *Excessive hostile verbalizations,* such as threats, scolds, and other negative comments directed toward the child (Burgess & Conger, 1978; Sandler *et al.*, 1978).
- *Excessive hostile physical gestures,* including pulling, slapping, or behaving as though one were going to slap the child (Wolfe *et al.*, 1982).

As these individual behaviors suggest, the therapist evaluating an interaction should attempt to assess (1) how effectively the parent uses positive attention (praise and physical affection) when the child behaves appropriately or follows directions; (2) whether the parent reacts appropriately to child misbehavior (by withdrawing attention, redirecting the child's actions, or restating a request) or inappropriately (by providing attention to misbehavior, or by scolding and threatening); (3) whether the parent's communications to the child are clear and appropriate to the child's age and comprehension level; and (4) whether the parent is attending sufficiently to the child's actions. Depending upon the therapist's aim and the degree of assessment quantification being sought, parent–child interactions can be objectively coded using various observational recording formats. While a detailed review of behavior coding systems and procedures is beyond the scope of this book, specialized descriptions of each can be found in other sources (cf. Forehand & McMahon, 1981; Patterson *et al.*, 1969).

4.4.4.3. Assessment of Child Behavior

Although attention is often focused on evidence of parent skill deficits during direct observations, it is also important for the therapist to evaluate carefully the child's behavior. Since such characteristics as hyperactivity, noncompliance, intellectual impairment, and "irritability" may be more frequent among abused children (Baldwin &

Oliver, 1975; Friedrich & Boriskin, 1976; Martin *et al.*, 1974), observation of the parent and child interaction can be used, in part, to assess their presence.

In addition, these sessions should include attention to the child's reactions to the parent. While research has traditionally emphasized the influence that parents exert on children, child behavior reciprocally determines parent responses (Bell, 1968). Thus, the therapist observing a parent–child interaction should evaluate whether the child follows or ignores parent commands, antagonizes the parent by hitting at him or her, responds to the parent's verbal praise, or appears to be reinforced by the parent's anger. Given that some children are more difficult to control than others, it is important that the clinician gauge how difficult it will be for the parent to manage the youngster. This will determine the type and intensity of later parent training intervention.

In summary, the purpose of child-management assessment is to determine whether injury to a child is a result of the parent's violent, corporal strategies for controlling child misbehavior. Interviews, inventory assessment, parent self-monitoring of problem behaviors, and direct observation of parent–child interactions can all provide data on the child's behavior and parent's current skills in handling misbehavior. If problems in child management are identified, later intervention to increase the parent's use of effective, nonviolent skills is needed.

4.5. ASSESSING PARENT KNOWLEDGE OF CHILD BEHAVIOR AND DEVELOPMENT

To this point, we have considered the assessment of a parent's child-management *skills*. A related assessment area that also merits attention is the parent's knowledge of children and, more specifically, knowledge of what to reasonably expect of youngsters the same age as the abused child. If a parent has unrealistically high developmental expectations for the youngster, he or she may experience frustration and anger when the child fails to meet those expectations.

Formal, structured measures that tap parent knowledge of child development have not yet been widely used with abusive families, and assessment in this area should be tailored to knowledge about children of the same age as the target child. During assessment interviews, and especially if the parent's comments indicate the presence of unrealistic expectations concerning the child, the following areas should be explored:

Does the parent have reasonable knowledge of typical "developmental milestones?" In one case seen in our clinic, an abusive parent reported feeling anger because her one-year-old child was not yet well toilet-trained. Other parents believe that their infants' nighttime crying is an unusual problem and the sign of a "bad" baby. Parents frequently appear to overestimate their children's developmental capacity for receptive and expressive communication, causing frustration when the youngster fails to communicate in a manner the parent expects. To the extent that parents, and especially inexperienced parents, lack knowledge of what children of a certain age *can* do, unrealistic expectations and parent–child conflicts may develop.

Does the parent incorrectly attribute malicious intent to the child? Normal parents, during times of difficulty with their children, must occasionally wonder if the child isn't "out to get them." When a parent experiences *repeated* management frustrations and lacks knowledge about children, it is possible for that individual to develop incorrect attributions that the youngster is attempting to provoke the parent intentionally and maliciously. While data on this issue are limited, several reports suggest that abusive parents are likely to develop such negative attributions concerning their children (Blumberg, 1974; Wasserman, 1967). If a parent incorrectly believes that a young child is intentionally trying to cause harm or frustration, or if a parent attributes other life difficulties to the presence of the child, these areas should be targeted for further discussion and intervention.

Are there unrealistic expectations concerning the child's ability to provide nurturance and understanding for the parent? Just as parents can overestimate their children's physical–developmental capabilities, they may also have unrealistic expectations concerning a child's capacity for emotional maturity and social supportiveness. In one case report (Scott *et al.*, 1982), episodes of child maltreatment were found to take place when the mother had angry disagreements with other adults and her child later misbehaved; the youngster's misbehavior, she reported, showed that the child lacked concern for her own interpersonal difficulties. In this case, one problem area was the parent's unrealistic expectation that a young child *could* exhibit concern for her difficulties. While the phenomenon of "role reversal" has generally been interpreted using psychoanalytic terms (Blumberg, 1974; Green *et al.*, 1974; Wasserman, 1967), it may simply reflect the parent's expectation of advanced emotionally and socially understanding responses that a child is unable to exhibit.

4.6. ASSESSMENT OF ANGER-CONTROL DEFICITS

Assessing and modifying parent anger responses is one of the most potentially important, but one of the least investigated, aspects of child abuse treatment. As Dubanowski *et al.* (1978) note, the vast majority of abuse incidents appear to occur when the parent is angry and in a state of emotional overarousal. While this argues for assessing and reducing the problems that lead to the parent's anger in the first place (such as child-management difficulties and SES stressors), it also suggests the importance of teaching parents to control their anger and emotional overarousal when confronted by difficult situations. In order to do this, the therapist must first assess the degree to which anger accompanies aggression toward the child, the specific situations which currently elicit anger, and the parent's present means of handling anger. We will now examine several ways to gain this information during client assessment sessions.

4.6.1. Interview Assessment of Anger

Dubanowski *et al.* (1978) point out that it is important not only to pinpoint specific problems the abusive parent experiences (whether these are management difficulties with the child or other life problems), but also to determine if the parent currently exhibits anger in those problem situations. In essence, this requires the therapist both to assess specific problem situations and to evaluate the anger or emotional "valence" of parental responses in those situations. As an example, the crying or tantrumming of a young child is a stimulus that may be highly aversive and anger-provoking to one parent but not to another. Since aggressive responses are more likely to occur when an individual has labeled himself or herself as "angry" (Bandura, 1973; Berkowitz, 1974; Wolfe *et al.*, in press), it is clinically important to delineate those problem situations that now elicit feelings of anger, frustration, or perceived loss of control. Based on this information, the therapist can develop a two-pronged intervention plan that (1) provides treatment to reduce the likelihood that the parent will continue to encounter these problems (such as child-management training if the difficulties involve handling the child's behavior) and (2) teaches anger-control and stress-coping skills to help the parent deal with anger should the problem situations recur in the future.

Just as carefully conducted interviews are the most practical way to assess a family's child-management problems initially, anger assessment can also begin with parent interviews. Verbal self-reports of anger can often be obtained at the same time the therapist is questioning the parent about various problems that s/he experiences. For example, in the previous section we discussed the assessment of child-management difficulties. Anger assessment can accompany this if the parent is questioned about his or her feelings and behavior when the child exhibits any misbehavior described as problematic. If the parent reports child tantrumming as a difficulty, the therapist might include questions about the parent's degree of anger and his or her anger-related behavior when the child has tantrums.

Although it is always important to assess the extent of parent anger toward the child when the child misbehaves, anger assessment should not be *limited* to interactions occurring between the parent and youngster. It is possible for other events in the parent's life, unrelated to the child, to induce anger or frustration; when the parent is in an overaroused state, even minor child misbehavior may serve to elicit aggression. In the study reported by Scott *et al.* (1982), careful interviews revealed that most instances of a mother's violent behavior toward her child occurred when the parent was angry following heated disagreements with her current boyfriend. In this case, some of the anger-inducing situations were frustrations outside the parent–child relationship. Anger assessment information can be obtained when the therapist discusses any problem situations experienced by the parent, including child-management difficulties and external family stressors (e.g., joblessness, interpersonal frustrations, marital difficulties, social isolation).

4.6.2. Self-Monitoring of Anger

Just as parents can be asked to record instances of child misbehavior to help the therapist pinpoint the type of child-management training that will later be needed, they can also self-monitor occasions when anger or stress are experienced. Using a self-monitoring form that is completed daily, parents might (1) note any times during that day when they felt anger or frustration; (2) assign a quantified numerical rating, such as by an anchored 1–10 scale, to indicate the degree of anger experienced in the situation; (3) provide a description of the episode that "caused" the anger; and (4) make a brief notation of how the anger was handled. Alternatively, information on anger can be integrated into the self-monitoring instrument used by the parent to record child-management problems. Here, the parent would mark a rating and description of his/her anger accompanying any notation of a child-management problem incident.

4.6.3. Physiological Assessment of Anger Arousal

As we noted in Chapter 2, several research investigations have utilized physiological and observational assessment measures to evaluate the responses of abusive parents when they are presented with aversive child stimuli such as crying and noncompliance (Disbrow *et al.*, 1977; Frodi & Lamb, 1980; Wolfe *et al.*, in press). Since abusive parents in these studies were found to exhibit signs of heightened or atypical anger arousal to cues of aversive child behavior, physiological assessment techniques may prove useful as a clinical assessment procedure. Dubanowski *et al.* (1978) suggest that potential elicitors of abuse (such as child crying, tantrumming, or other aversive stimuli) might be presented while the parent's arousal level, including heart-rate, breathing, skin conductance, is physiologically monitored. Stimuli which elicit heightened arousal can be the focus of anger-control intervention (e.g., by teaching the parent to use physical and cognitive relaxation techniques when the child emits the targeted aversive behaviors).

The chief advantage of physiological assessment lies in its ability to detect arousal independent of the parent's self-reports of anger. Especially for parents who appear to become extremely angry and agitated to cues of child misbehavior, the fine-grained physiological assessment of specific arousal patterns may be quite useful both to evaluate parent responses before intervention and, later, to evaluate reductions in arousal following treatment. The primary disadvantage of physiological techniques is that they have been used with abusive parents only in preliminary, group design assessment research and not yet as a part of clinical treatment studies. Normative data on the degree of arousal shown by *normal* parents to aversive child stimuli is largely unavailable, making the arousal shown by an abusive parent difficult to interpret clinically. In addition, some abusive parents, especially those who begin treatment hesitantly following a social welfare department investigation, can be frightened by the appearance of physiological recording apparatus. However, because physiological measures have proven useful in the assessment and treatment of other types of anger-control problems (cf. Novaco, 1975, 1976), exploration of their utility with child-abusive parents certainly merits further clinical attention.

4.7. ASSESSMENT OF FAMILY STRESSORS AND OTHER RISK FACTORS

In Chapters 2 and 3, life-style stressors that have been associated with an increased incidence of child abuse were discussed. However, it is important to reiterate that while stress factors such as joblessness, SES stress, marital discord, parent interpersonal difficulties, and social isolation have all been reported to occur disproportionately more often among abusive families, the research on which these findings are based is subject to methodological limitations, and studies have not yet demonstrated a direct, specific *causal* relationship between family stress and child abuse. Rather, and as proposed by Gil (1975), one can view stress factors as "context" variables which may create frustration and decrease general adaptive functioning and effective problem-solving.

Based on parent interviews, caseworker reports of the family's economic and interpersonal circumstances, and observations of the family that are made during any home visit, the therapist should assess the presence of family stressors and develop initial formulations concerning their possible relationship to abuse. Areas for evaluation include:

- *Joblessness.* Is the parent who would normally work unemployed? Does the period of unemployment coincide with the occurrence of increased violence within the family?
- *Inadequate financial resources.* Even if employed, are the income and financial resources of the family adequate to meet the family's needs? If not, does the period of increased financial stress coincide with increased family violence?
- *Inadequate child care resources.* Does the abusive parent appear "overwhelmed" by excessive child care responsibilities, with too many children for whom to care and few alternative resources for child care assistance (other adults, daycare center)? Does the parent report this as a stressor that increases feelings of anger or frustration?
- *Marital conflict.* If both parents are present in the family, do the parents report a problem of serious marital discord or conflict? If marital difficulties exist, are the couple's arguments characterized by physical violence between spouses and toward children in the family? Are episodes of child-directed violence in any way temporally related to disagreements between the parents?
- *Parent relationship difficulties with others.* Does the abusive parent report difficulties or frustrations when dealing with others, such as relatives, friends, co-workers, or dates? If present, do such difficulties elicit anger and cause the parent to be more

easily irritated by the child? Did past periods of child-directed violence occur when the parent was angry or frustrated with others?

- *Parent social isolation.* What is the extent and quality of the abusive parent's social support network outside the family? Does s/he have friends and, if so, does the parent engage in gratifying activities with them? Is the parent able to leave child care responsibilities to participate in social activities with others? Or, in contrast, is the parent socially isolated and "insular" (Wahler, 1980)?

While stress factors such as these are probably neither necessary nor sufficient in themselves to produce child-abusive behavior within most families, they may well enhance the probability of child-directed violence and other coping difficulties within the family (Gil, 1970; 1975). In addition, many of these stressors, if unalleviated, could limit the effectiveness of other more specific forms of intervention. For example, if training in child-management skills is indicated, but a parent is continually overwhelmed by the presence of many children with no alternative child care arrangemetns, it may prove difficult to implement effective child-management programs. Until it is possible to define more accurately the antecedents and contributors toward child-abusive behavior within individual families, it is reasonable for therapists to scrutinize, and develop a plan to remediate, stress variables that may place the family at higher risk for continued violence.

4.8. INTEGRATING ASSESSMENT DATA INTO A TREATMENT INTERVENTION PLAN

Based upon the information obtained during a family's assessment, it is usually possible to identify specific areas that will require intervention. Adopting the organization followed in this chapter, we can conceptualize potential treatment areas to include:

- *Training parents to use nonviolent methods of child discipline* if assessment indicates that instances of abuse can be traced to the use of overly harsh, physically punitive means of controlling misbehavior.

- *Teaching parents to utilize positive reinforcement-based child-management techniques,* reducing the need to discipline the child and establishing more positive interactions between the parent and youngster.
- *Teaching anger-control and stress-management skills* if episodes of child-directed violence are characterized by parent anger and loss of self-control.
- *Intervening to reduce life-style risk factors and family stressors* that appear functionally, if indirectly, related to the parent's episodes of violence. Depending upon the factors identified during a family's assessment, this might include attention to reducing marital conflict, assisting the parent in job finding or budgeting, developing alternative child care arrangements such as daycare, or helping the parent develop more frequent or more gratifying social relationships with other adults.

While it is possible that a family will require treatment in only a single problem area, it appears more common for child-abusive families to experience multiple difficulties that, in turn, require several types of intervention (Friedman *et al.*, 1981; Scott *et al.*, 1982). If this is the case, it may prove desirable for the therapist to prioritize components of treatment, with attention first directed to those areas that are most immediately related to episodes of child-directed violence. Thus, one parent might first receive a series of skills-training sessions to teach alternatives to physical punishment, with concurrent attention to the development of positive reinforcement-based child-management skills. In later sessions, specific training in anger-control techniques might be an additional focus of intervention. The specific areas to receive treatment attention, the pace of intervention, and whether different problem areas are addressed sequentially or concurrently in treatment will depend on the therapist's assessment findings and the ability of the parents to show behavior change.

4.8.1. Establishing a Therapy Contract with the Abusive Parent

Earlier in this chapter, we noted that abusive parents often begin treatment under less than voluntary circumstances, such as in response to a court order, to regain unsupervised custody of their child, or as the result of a child-protective agency recommendation. When intervention is mandated or directed, rather than voluntarily requested by a family, there is a potential for misunderstandings concerning the purpose and reasons for treatment. Since a parent's immediate goals (to regain custody of the child without perceived "interference" by child-protective workers) may be different than the therapist's or agency's goals (to ensure the child's safety and reduce the risk of violence), it is important for all parties to establish a consensual understanding about the nature of treatment and the manner in which a family's participation in therapy is related to the social welfare agency's actions with regard to the child.

4.8.1.1. Establishing a Contract between the Therapist and the Family

The use of therapy contracts is relatively common in both psychological and social work interventions (Stein, Gambrill, & Wiltse, 1974; Weiss, Hops, & Patterson, 1973; Wolfe *et al.*, 1981a). The purpose of a treatment contract is to make explicit the goals and nature of therapy, and to clarify the responsibilities of both the client (in this case, the parent or family) and the therapist. Often, a time frame for periodic treatment assessment is also specified; this might mean that after every fifth session, progress and remaining difficulties are reviewed by the therapist and the client.

Following a family's assessment, and when the therapist has determined those problem areas that will require attention, an outline of the planned intervention should be presented to the family. This can include a description of specific, identified problem areas and types of skills training that will be covered in treatment, requests that will be made of the parents (e.g., to practice new ways of handling their children at home), and the frequency and scheduling of sessions.

Therapy contracts may be formalized in writing or they can be handled less formally, with discussion and agreement on these matters between the therapist and parent. In either case, efforts should be made to elicit parental suggestions concerning difficulties that are perceived as problematic. Especially if a parent does not appear to understand why s/he has been requested to attend sessions, the concrete benefits of treatment can be explained (e.g., the parent will learn to handle his or her children more effectively or ways to deal with anger will be taught).

4.8.1.2. Establishing Contracts among the Therapist, Parent, and Social Welfare Agency

When a family is directed or ordered to treatment by court or social welfare authorities, it is usually with the implicit threat that nonparticipation will result in some negative consequence for the parents. If the child has been removed from the home, the parent may be told that the youngster will not be returned until intervention is made. Unfortunately, as Wolfe *et al.* (1981a) point out, there is often a lack of specific communication among welfare authorities, therapists, and parents about what constitutes acceptable progress in treatment, as well as the contingencies for attending or not attending sessions.

Many of these difficulties can be reduced if a contractual approach is used in overall case planning. While the exact nature of the contract will vary across families, efforts should be made to specify (1) *what is being requested of the parents* (e.g., to attend sessions weekly); (2) *how information on the parents' participation will be communicated to social welfare or legal authorities* (e.g., the therapist will provide monthly reports describing the number of sessions attended, the treatment areas covered, and evidence of behavior change); (3) *what positive benefits to the family will occur as they participate in sessions* (e.g., the frequency and duration of home visits by a formerly removed child will be increased on a prearranged schedule during the time the family is receiving treatment); and (4) *what negative consequences will occur if the parents do not participate* (e.g., home visits will be suspended and the family's states reevaluated by authorities). Wolfe *et al.* (1981a) suggest that time frames for accomplishing treatment goals also be established. This could include setting a definite time period for formal case reevaluation (such as following the eighth or tenth treatment session) at which point welfare authority involvement in the family's affair might be decreased (contingent on successful parent participation) or maintained (contingent on unsuccessful participation). To the extent that the responsibilities of the parents, the therapist, and social–judicial authorities are made explicit, progress toward returning the child safely to the sole custody of his or her parents can also be evaluated more accurately and without misunderstandings.

Finally, we have focused attention in this chapter on methods for assessing clients before treatment begins. All of the measures and techniques described here can be used not only to determine those problem areas that will require intervention, but also to assess progress and behavior change during treatment. Therapists may wish to evaluate improvement periodically by readministering inventories, reassessing the presence or severity of life-style stressors, analyzing changes in the parent's self-monitoring records of anger or child-management problems, and conducting home visits to assess whether parents are applying new child-management skills (and whether the child's behavior changes in response to them). To the extent that a therapist evaluates the impact of an intervention using multiple and relatively objective criteria, it is possible to determine more conclusively whether meaningful change is taking place. We will turn our attention now to intervention techniques with these families.

5

Training Abusive Parents to Use Nonviolent Child Discipline Strategies

When family assessment indicates that parents are relying on excessively harsh corporal punishment to control child misbehavior, and especially if instances of child injury are traceable to the parent's use of extremely punitive discipline, training in appropriate, nonviolent child-management skills is needed. Essentially, the therapist seeks to assist the parent in replacing current violent forms of discipline (such as excessive screaming, spanking, hitting, or beating) with more effective management skills that are nonviolent in nature. As the parent uses these appropriate skills to deal with child misbehavior, the risk of violence, and therefore injury, during disciplinary episodes will be reduced. Although we will focus in this chapter on strategies for assisting parents to handle *misbehavior* nonviolently, a closely related clinical task is helping parents to use positive-reinforcement-based techniques simultaneously when interacting with their children. That topic will be discussed in Chapter 6, and therapists will always want to combine attention to reducing a parent's violent disciplinary practices with concurrent attention to teaching more positive interaction skills. In this way, treatment extends beyond the short-term goal of reducing a parent's current reliance on harsh discipline to the longer-range goal of establishing positive reinforcement-based interactions within the family.

Before we turn our attention to specific child-management techniques that can be taught to abusive parents, several more general treatment-related issues also merit our discussion. These include possible reasons why parents use violent disciplinary practices and may be reluctant to alter their current style of discipline, and dealing with parents' attitudinal beliefs that harsh physical punishment is an appropriate form of discipline. Since parents are most likely to learn and apply new skills that they genuinely believe are useful and appropriate, attention to these preliminary issues can enhance the likelihood that parent-training efforts will be successful.

5.1. FACTORS INFLUENCING THE USE OF PHYSICAL PUNISHMENT: PREPARING PARENTS FOR CHILD-MANAGEMENT TRAINING

When we reviewed a social-learning conceptualization of child abuse, several factors were presented that can account for certain parents' reliance on corporal punishment to control child misbehavior. A parent's own observational learning history (e.g., being raised by parents who used similar practices) is one influence on how the parent will behave toward his or her own children. The standards or behavior modeled and reinforced by "significant others" in the parent's life (such as neighbors, relatives, or friends) is another influence. However, a more immediate, relevant factor that can account for physically punitive child-management styles is the parent's personal experience that punishment *does* suppress misbehavior, at least on a short-term basis. While we raised this as a theoretical/conceptual issue in Chapter 3, it is also an important clinical issue that should be explored with families prior to the introduction of child-management training. Until a parent is aware that there are techniques not only more appropriate but also more *effective* than spanking or hitting, it is unlikely that the individual will seriously apply new, alternative management skills.

5.1.1. Reviewing with Parents When Spanking Is Appropriate

There is clearly a range of opinions, even among psychologists and family therapists, about when (or even whether) spanking is appropriate. However, from a practical standpoint, most parents (including nonabusive normal parents) probably feel that spanking is justified and necessary at certain times and, if they have this belief, instructions to *never* spank a child are likely to be disregarded and the therapist's overall credibility questioned.

In our clinic, parents are told that it is permissible to spank children, but only under very specific circumstances and in a clearly prescribed manner. Spanking is first defined operationally as a single "swat" with an open palm on the child's buttocks. Parents are told that multiple spanks, hitting with any object or with anything other than an open palm, spanks anywhere other than on the child's bottom, shaking, and similarly violent behaviors are never acceptable under any circumstance. The use of spanking by abusive parents is largely limited to occasions when the child is engaging in an activity that is dangerous and cannot be tolerated for that reason. Parents are told, for example, that it is appropriate to administer one spank if a child is about to run into the street, attempts to pull a hot skillet from the stove, or so on. However, they are instructed to refrain from spanking at other times and told to use, instead, other management techniques that will be presented later in this chapter.

Therapists treating child-abusive parents may be understandably concerned about permitting the parent to utilize any form of physical discipline. On the other hand, it is probably unrealistic to suggest (or expect) that abusive parents will never spank their children, especially since almost all normal parents do spank on at least an occasional basis (Gelles, 1978). From a clinical perspective, a more useful approach may be providing parents with specific albeit conservative and closely monitored guidelines on when they can spank, what behavior constitutes a spank (as opposed to a beating), and how to use techniques other than spanking. The overall aim of child-management training is not to prevent an abusive parent from disciplining his or her child; instead, it is to teach the parent to handle misbehavior appropriately, to discriminate among situations when various management techniques are needed, and to improve the quality of interactions between family members.

5.1.2. Providing Information on the Disadvantages of Frequent Spanking

Although occasional spanking for certain child misbehaviors, such as engaging in potentially dangerous acts, is common among most parents and is defensible, the assessment of abusive families may indicate that corporal, harsh punishment is being used in too frequent, too indiscriminate, or too intense a manner. If a parent has learned to control child misbehavior through excessively punitive responses, it is important to review with the parent reasons why spanking, hitting, beating and other similar forms of punishment are both inappropriate and ineffective.

The research literature on punishment and behavior control has yielded a number of scientific findings that can be "translated" into simplified explanations that most parents can understand. When discussing why a parent's current punitive disciplinary practices are ineffective or are failing to produce durable change in the chi;d's behavior, the following commonsense explanations may be presented:

1. *Physical punishment like spanking can control a child's misbehavior, but its results are often temporary*. Thus, the parent may find that s/he has to repeatedly punish the child for the same actions.
2. *While physical punishment tells a child what not to do, it does not guide the child in learning improved behavior*. This again leads to the effect of temporarily suppressing misbehavior without producing enduring improvement in the child's actions.
3. *Children acclimate to corporal punishment, so discipline loses its effectiveness*. As this acclimation takes place, the parent who relies primarily on physical punishment may find that s/he has to discipline more harshly to achieve any effect. Risk of serious injury to the child increases as the intensity of punishment increases.
4. *Because spanking is unpleasant for most parents, the frequent use of corporal punishment creates a frustrating, negative, and stressful*

home atmosphere for everyone involved. Forms of discipline that are not physically punitive are more effective and more conducive to calm, positive family interactions.

5. *Frequent use of harsh physical punishment is more likely to result in fear than respect for the parent.*

While these are simplified explanations of what are really complex behavioral phenomena (see, for example, discussions of punishment by Azrin, 1958; Azrin *et al.*, 1963; Reynolds, 1975), they can be presented to most parents quite easily. We have also found it useful to encourage parents to discuss the specific problems they encounter when using corporal punishment with their children (e.g., the child misbehaves a short time later, punishment has little apparent effect, the parent feels bad when disciplining the child). To the extent that parents are able to identify disadvantages to their current punitive practices, they will be more open to acquiring new management skills.

5.1.3. Recognizing That Some Parents Have Attitudinal Beliefs Favoring the Use of Harsh Corporal Punishment

Parents who rely on frequent physical punishment to control misbehavior may believe that this is an appropriate child-management style. Thus, while a parent may regret that his or her child was injured during a disciplinary episode, the parent may still believe that his or her basic style of handling misbehavior with strong punishment is appropriate and correct. From a cognitive–behavioral perspective, parents can develop attitudes favoring the use of physical punishment in several ways. Since personal exposure to violent models increases one's own tolerance concerning the acceptability of violence (Berkowitz, 1962; Felsenthal, 1976; Lovaas, 1961), parents who were themselves exposed to harsh parental models would be likely to view this disciplinary style as correct and acceptable. Attitudes are also influenced by one's own past behavior; if a parent routinely handles child misbehavior using physical punishment, that parent's cognitive attitudes concerning the appropriateness of spanking or hitting are likely to be consistent with his or her own actions (Brown, 1965; Festinger, 1957). Finally, some abusive parents appear to be influenced, on a cognitive–attitudinal level, by "folk wisdom" that it is necessary to be stern and punishment-oriented with one's children. "Spare the rod, spoil the child," the belief that harsh punishment "builds respect," or even certain religious views stressing the need to punish a child's sins and transgressions harshly can all reinforce an attitudinal system favoring the use of excessive punishment toward children (see discussions by Korbin, 1977, and Burgess, 1979).

While altering and challenging a parent's attitudes concerning the appropriateness of frequent physical punishment appear to be important components of intervention, this topic has received very little attention or even recognition in the parent-training literature. From a clinical point of view, one would expect that enduring behavior change will be produced only if a parent believes that new skills to be taught are more desirable, appropriate, and acceptable than those actions currently practiced. For this reason, efforts should be made to assess and, if necessary, to challenge beliefs that one must be punitive to be a "good parent." However, before parents can evaluate alternative methods for child management, they must first acquire new skills for handling troublesome situations with their children. We will now turn our attention to training parents in alternatives to physical punishment for handling misbehavior.

5.2. TRAINING PARENTS IN THE USE OF TIME OUT AS AN ALTERNATIVE TO VIOLENT FORMS OF DISCIPLINE

Time out is a child-management procedure that has been studied and applied successfully in a wide range of interventions with parents and their children. The term "time out" refers to the removal of a child, for a relatively short period of time, from sources of attention and reinforcement contingent upon a misbehavior of some type. As Sulzer-Azaroff and Mayer (1977) point out, variations of time out are used quite commonly and informally by many parents; sending a child to his room for fighting with a sibling, requiring a youngster to sit on a bench for ten minutes after pushing another child into a swimming pool, or telling a child to stand alone in a hallway for a short period of time following a classroom misbehavior are all variations of the time out principle. In each example, the consequence of a child's undesirable behavior is brief removal or isolation from the setting where the misbehavior occurred and where reinforcement takes place. Since sitting alone on a bench, standing by oneself in a hallway, or spending time alone in a room are all dull and nonreinforcing and provide little attention, most children find periods spent in time out to be unpleasant. Importantly, the value of time out is that it changes behavior through the temporary removal of positive reinforcement, rather than by the application of physical punishment.

While informal removal-from-reinforcement techniques are used occasionally by most parents, time out as a clinical intervention is much more consistent, specific, and clearly defined. When implemented in a carefully planned manner, time out has been shown effective for reducing children's disruptive and aggressive behavior, tantrums, verbal outbursts, fighting, and severe noncompliance (Benoit & Mayer, 1975; Bostow & Bailey, 1969; Wolf, Risley, Johnson, Harris, & Allen, 1967; Zeilberger, Sampen, & Sloane, 1968). Since these types of misbehaviors are often otherwise handled by physical punishment, training abusive parents in the use of time out provides a method for them to control a range of relatively serious child misbehaviors in a nonviolent manner.

5.2.1. Teaching Parents to Use Time Out Correctly

Time out can best be viewed as a nonviolent alternative to spanking. This implies that the use of time out should be focused on such "serious" misbehaviors as tantrumming, aggression, or direct noncompliance with reasonable requests made by the parent. The specific problems to be targeted by time out within a given family are, of course, determined by careful assessment of child behavior problems and the parents' current methods for dealing with them. If a parent is unable to control his or her child's serious misbehaviors, or if the parent's current methods of control involve corporal or explosive punishment, this management skill is often appropriate.

While there are some procedural variations in the implementation of time out, the following steps are relatively standard for teaching parents to use the technique:

5.2.1.1. Specific Misbehaviors That Will Result in Time Out Are Identified with the Parent

Before time out is implemented, it is important to review the data on child misbehavior obtained during the family assessment phase, including child behavior problem checklists, monitoring records completed by the parent, and information gained during interviews on parent–child interactions. Time out is not an "all purpose" strategy for handling any type of child-management problem; instead, its use is focused on only a limited number of serious misbehaviors (such as fighting, tantrumming, or direct noncompliance) that should be *reduced*. Time out is not used for more routine misbehaviors, and is never threatened in order to "motivate" the child to do something positive. Other reinforcement-based techniques, especially those we will discuss in the next chapter, are used to increase desirable behavior.

5.2.1.2. A Time Out Location in the Home Is Selected

The ideal location is a quiet place, removed from family activities and other diversions, where the child will be sent for time out. A spare room, a corner of the hallway, or a bathroom that is first "child-proofed" by removing any dangerous objects or materials are all acceptable as time out locations. A time out spot should not have interesting diversions, such as toys, games, or a television; it should be sufficiently isolated from family activities that the child will be effectively removed from possible sources of social attention. On the other hand, the location should never be frightening or emotionally upsetting; dark rooms, closets, or places the child fears are never acceptable locations. The main requirement is that the time out spot simply be dull and isolated from activities the child enjoys.

5.2.1.3. Time Out Immediately Follows the Targeted Misbehavior

If time out is being used to control a child's tantrums, the parent is instructed to tell the child calmly but firmly that s/he will have to go to the time out location if the tantrum continues. If the parent's instruction to stop is not heeded, time out immediately follows without any discussion other than a one-sentence explanation of why time out is being used. For other forms of misbehavior, the same procedure is followed: one request asking the child to stop engaging in the misbehavior, which if unheeded is quickly followed by time out.

5.2.1.4. Time Out Is for a Brief but Defined Period

Most studies indicate that a five- to ten-minute interval of time out is effective, and is more effective than longer periods which permit a child's adaptation and satiation to being in time out (see Sulzer-Azaroff & Mayer, 1977, for a discussion of this issue). Young children under four should spend five minutes in time out, while a ten-minute period is used for older children. If the parent instructs a child to go to time out and the child physically resists being escorted by the parent to the location, the child should be told that two more minutes will be added to the time out period. After two such time extensions have been added, the child resisting time out should be calmly and unemotionally taken to the location by the parent.

As soon as the child enters the time out location, timing of the interval to be spent there begins. It is useful for parents to place a timer with a bell, such as an ordinary kitchen timer, near the location so the number of minutes can be accurately set. When the bell rings, the end of time out is signalled to both the parent and the child.

In most applications by parents, the basic time period of five to ten minutes is extended only if the child refuses to go to time out (when two extra two-minute periods are added), if the child continues to tantrum excessively once in time (in which case the timed period begins when the child has become relatively quiet), or if the child leaves the time out area (resulting in the original period being reset). Longer intervals in time out should never be used to punish the child.

5.2.1.5. No Social Interaction Occurs with a Child in Time Out; After Time Out Is Over, the Disciplinary Episode Is Completed

Parents or family members should be instructed to avoid interacting with the child in time out, since attention negates the value of the technique. If the parent's level of anger or arousal is high, the period when the child is in time out is also an ideal time for the parent to engage in self-relaxation and anger-coping skills (as described in Chapter 7). When the child's time out has ended, parents should be told to consider the entire disciplinary episode completed. The therapist can remind the parent that time out replaces spanking, scolding, or even discussing the child's misbehavior after the episode is over. Therefore, all of these other disciplinary steps are discontinued when time out is used.

5.2.1.6. Consistency in Using Time Out Must Be Stressed to Parents

For time out to reduce misbehavior effectively, it must be used consistently by parents whenever the child engages in a misbehavior being targeted by this technique (e.g., tantrumming, fighting). After parents begin using time out, close contact should be maintained between the therapist and the parents to ensure that it is being used consistently and in the prescribed manner, to determine that the parent is not overextending the use of time out to behaviors for which it is not an appropriate management technique, and to reinforce the parent for using time out instead of violent disciplinary controls.

5.2.1.7. Whenever Time Out Is Being Used, a Program to Reinforce Desirable Behavior Should Be Concurrently Implemented

A basic principle in child-management training is that whenever any technique, including time out or other extinction-based procedures, is being used to decrease child misbehaviors, attention should be simultaneously directed toward increasing and reinforcing appropriate, desirable behavior from the child. This is particularly relevant for abusive families, where the clinical aim of child-management training is not merely to teach parents new ways to nonviolently discipline their children, but also to develop a positive-reinforcement-based management and interaction style. Approaches and techniques for teaching parents these positive reinforcement skills will be presented in detail in Chapter 6; therapists should always train parents in at least one of these techniques when they are instructed to begin using time out to control misbehaviors.

The steps outlined above represent the essential elements that should be covered when time out is taught to parents. There are, of course, variations and additional steps that can be taken to extend time-out-like procedures to cover other situations, such as extreme child behavior problems that occur outside the family's home, or unusual practical difficulties in implementing the technique, such as the absence of any suitable location for time out or extremely agitated behavior when the child is in time out. The therapist unfamiliar with variations in time out that can be used to handle these problems may wish to consult a more specialized resource for information (see Benoit & Mayer, 1975; Bostow & Bailey, 1969; Sulzer-Azaroff & Mayer, 1977; Zeilberger *et al.*, 1968).

5.2.2. Training Abusive Parents to Use Time Out: Representative Research and Clinical Considerations

A number of interventions with abusive families have specifically taught parents to use time out for handling their children's serious misbehavior (Crimmins *et al.*, 1982; Crozier & Katz, 1979; Scott *et al.*, 1982; Wolfe *et al.*, 1982; Wolfe, Sandler, & Kaufman, 1981c). In all of these studies, time out was only one element of a more comprehensive training "package," and other skills to reduce child misbehavior (by ignoring or withdrawal of attention, appropriate punishment) and increase desirable child behavior (by positive reinforcement, contingent attention and praise, shaping) were also covered. This is consistent with our earlier observation that while time out is often a necessary component of effective child management, its use should always be in conjunction with other more positive behavior management techniques.

Training in the use of time out has been accomplished in three ways: by detailed instruction to abusive parents in how to use the technique, by the assignment of readings, and by therapist modeling of time out. Instructions should include not only a step-by-step description of the time out procedure itself, but also detailed information to help the parent discriminate when to use time out versus other management techniques. If an abusive parent is likely to have anger-control difficulties, care should be taken to ensure that s/he does not inappropriately "overuse" time out, extend the time that the child is in time out, or incorrectly define a minor child misbehavior as one that should result in time out. It is useful to ask parents to monitor all occasions when the procedure is used and to bring their monitoring records to therapy sessions so the therapist can review how time out is being implemented.

Several books, written at a level that makes them suitable for most parents, describe the use of behavioral child-management techniques including time out. *Solving Your Child's Behavior Problems* (Kelly, 1983), *Parents Are Teachers* (Becker, 1971), and *Living With Children* (Patterson, 1974) include descriptions of the handling of common behavior problems and can be used as assigned readings in conjunction with parent-training sessions. Such readings have been incorporated in several interventions with abusive families (Crozier & Katz, 1979; Denicola & Sandler, 1980; Wolfe & Sandler, 1981).

Finally, therapist modeling of time out can also be used to demonstrate to parents how this technique is carried out. In the Wolfe *et al.* (1982) project, observations of parent–child interactions were made in a clinic playroom. Occasionally, one of the children engaged in a seriously disruptive behavior (screaming or tantrumming) during interactions in this setting. On such occasions, the therapist modeled the actual use of time out for the parent; later, the parent implemented time out under the therapist's observation. If it is possible for the therapist to be present when a serious child misbehavior takes place (ideally, in the family's home or, alternatively, within the clinic setting), the therapist has the opportunity to model this management technique.

Training abusive parents to use time out broadens the parent's repertoire for dealing with serious child misbehaviors nonviolently. Another parent-training strategy for reducing misbehavior the parent is presently unable to control involves learning to remove attention contingent upon undesirable child behavior. We will now consider training parents in this technique.

5.3. TRAINING PARENTS TO USE ATTENTION WITHDRAWAL AS A CHILD-MANAGEMENT TECHNIQUE

A very basic principle in the applied child behavior analysis literature is that the conduct of children is influenced by its social consequences: actions which elicit social attention tend to be maintained, while those which fail to elicit attention or reinforcement decrease in frequency. With respect to parent–child interactions, the same principle holds true; the manner in which a parent reacts to a child's behavior is an important determinant of whether the behavior will persist, increase, or decrease in the future. To the extent that parental attention is reinforcing to a child, actions which elicit that attention will be maintained. Further, a number of investigators have reported that even what appear to be "negative" forms of attention (such as scolding, reprimands, and yelling) can function as reinforcers that strengthen misbehavior (Miller, 1980; Patterson, 1977). This is especially likely when a child receives very little "positive" attention from the parent, and when the primary means to elicit attention is engaging in a misbehavior.

Interestingly, descriptions of abusive families provide evidence that these parents inadvertently reinforce their children's continued misbehavior. The Burgess and Conger (1977a) study, discussed earlier, found that abusive parents exceed nonabusive parents in their use of negative verbal comments and fall below nonabusive parents in their rate of positive comments during at-home interactions. Since reprimands, scolds, and similar negative statements would ordinarily follow what the parent feels is a misbehavior, the excess use of such comments (especially in the relative absence of positive comments contingent on good child behavior) suggests that misbehavior is being maintained by negative attention. Case study analyses of parent–child interactions in playroom and home settings have also confirmed the presence of high-rate negative verbal attention by abusive parents when their children engage in inappropriate behavior, coupled with very low rates of positive attention for desirable child behavior (Crimmins *et al.*, 1982; Denicola & Sandler, 1980; Wolfe *et al.*,

1982). Finally, there have been occasional, albeit uncontrolled, observations that some abused children appear to seek out negative attention and reactions from their parents (Kempe & Kempe, 1976). While this phenomenon has often been accounted for in psychoanalytic terms, it may indicate that the child has learned that s/he can elicit a parent attentional response of *some* kind through misbehavior and that the likelihood of obtaining social reinforcement for desirable behavior in the family is low.

In the previous section, we described the process of teaching parents to use time out as a nonviolent way to handle serious child misbehaviors. Since the rationale of time out entails removing a child from sources of attention contingent on unacceptable behavior, it is actually a structured attention- or reinforcement-withdrawal procedure. Parents can also be taught to alter selectively their attention, without implementing a formal time out, in order to reduce misbehaviors that are currently being maintained by attention.

5.3.1. Determining When to Use Attention Withdrawal Procedures

As one would expect, attention removal is most effective as a child-management skill when the misbehavior a parent seeks to reduce is being maintained by social reinforcement from the parent. In the treatment of a clinical case, it may be difficult to determine conclusively all of the reinforcers operating to maintain a child's behavior. However, implementation of parent training in attention withdrawal should be considered if (1) assessment data, including information derived from parent interviews and direct therapist observation of parent–child interactions, suggest that the parent provides excessive social attention when the child misbehaves; (2) the child's misbehavior is maintained or increases following the parent's usual response; or (3) the child appears to be "provoking" intentionally and successfully an emotional reaction from the parent. In general, removal of attention is an appropriate technique for managing child misbehaviors less serious than those which would result in time out, although simple attention withdrawal has been successfully used to reduce children's tantrums and overtly aggressive actions (Carlson, Arnold, Becker, & Madsen, 1968; Scott, Burton, & Yarrow, 1967; Wolf, Risley, & Mees, 1964).

5.3.2. Teaching Parents to Use Attention Withdrawal Correctly

Just as the implementation of time out begins by delineating specific misbehaviors that are to be handled by that technique rather than by spanking, it is important to use a family's assessment data to identify specific child-management problems that can be handled through contingent removal of parent attention. Examples of target behaviors appropriate for intervention with attention removal might include crying when it is clearly manipulative rather than an indication of a child's actual fear or distress; inappropriate disruptive actions to gain the parent's attention; "talking back" or cursing; and minor tantrumming. To monitor the effectiveness of the intervention and to ensure that it is being used appropriately, the therapist should instruct the parent to apply attention removal to only a single undesirable child behavior or a very limited number of behaviors at a time. Later, after the parent gains skill in using attention selectively, s/he can extend it to other child-management problems that occur.

When the therapist has identified child misbehaviors that will be targeted for attention, the following points (adapted from Becker, 1971; Kelly, 1983; Sulzer-Azaroff & Mayer, 1977) can be carefully reviewed with the parent.

5.3.2.1. A Detailed Rationale for Attention Withdrawal Is Presented

Most parents intuitively understand that children do things to "get attention." Following from this, parents can be told that *removing* attention when a child misbehaves is an effective way to control behavior problems. It is also important to stress that responses a parent considers to be punishing—such as scolding, yelling, or losing one's temper—can actually function as attention which reinforces children's continued misbehavior. Finally, parents sometimes feel that by not responding to a misbehavior they are conveying acceptance or encouragement to the child; this incorrect belief may need to be corrected by the therapist. To the extent that parents clearly understand the rationale for attention withdrawal, they will be able to apply it more effectively.

5.3.3. Attention Removal Is Applied Selectively and Consistently

If a child inappropriately whines and loudly shouts to get his mother's attention, and if this behavior angers and frustrates the parent, it is a logical target for intervention. In this case, the parent would be instructed to cease responding in any visible way when the child engages in whining or shouting activity. Verbal comments, responding to the child, reprimands, eye contact, or displays of anger all constitute aspects of attention that can reinforce the undesirable behavior. For this procedure to be effective, all attentional parent responses must be eliminated when the undesirable child behavior occurs.

5.3.3.1. Withdrawal of Attention Is Brief and Is Always Coupled with Extra Attention for Appropriate Behavior

Removal of attention should be used only while the child is actually engaging in the identified misbehavior and for a short period (usually under one minute) following the termination of the misbehavior. Extended, indiscriminate ignoring is never acceptable, both for ethical reasons and because protracted nonattention is an ineffective behavior change technique. Parents can be encouraged to think of their attention as a resource that is dispensed contingently: no attention (including negative attention) is provided when the child misbehaves, while extra and positive attention is given when the child resumes behaving appropriately.

This leads us to another critical aspect of parent training. Whenever parents use an attention-removal technique, they should always incorporate with it a method to provide extra attention and reinforcement for appropriate child behavior. In its most simple form, parents can be taught to initiate positive interactions with their children when the misbehavior incident and brief attention-removal phase are over.

Feedback ("Tommy, I like it better when you don't shout when you get mad"), instruction to the child ("Just come up and tell me what is wrong instead of tantrumming"), and praise ("You're a good boy when you don't throw tantrums") can all be used by parents as positive forms of attention that enhance the development of appropriate behavior patterns. Child-management techniques for increasing positive child behavior will be discussed in detail in the next chapter. At this point, it is important for the therapist to be aware of the need to teach parents to use positive attention to shape children's desirable behavior concurrent with parent training in attention withdrawal techniques.

5.3.3.2. *Possible Child Responses to Attention Withdrawal Should Be Reviewed*

When parents begin implementing withdrawal, a period of increased misbehavior (termed a "response burst") often occurs (Kelly, 1969). Youngsters often learn, over a considerable period of time, that they can gain attention through certain actions. When the parent first stops attending to inappropriate behavior, the child may increase (in frequency or intensity) misbehavior simply because it has been reinforced in the past. As long as the parent consistently maintains the strategy of ignoring the misbehavior, even if it temporarily worsens, there will be a progressive decline in the child's screaming. It is important to forewarn parents to anticipate a temporary worsening in their child's behavior when attention is removed, and to instruct them to continue handling the targeted misbehavior consistently until it improves. Parents should also be asked to maintain monitoring records of the child's rate of misbehavior so the therapist and parent can accurately assess the shorter- and longer-term effects of the intervention.

5.3.3.3. *Anger-Control Skills May Be Needed in Management Problem Situations*

When the use of time out was discussed, we noted that parents who become angry can be taught self-calming or anger-management skills and encouraged to use these coping strategies while the child is in time out. Since several studies indicate that abusive individuals exhibit atypical arousal when presented with cues of even relatively common forms of aversive child behavior (Frodi & Lamb, 1980; Wolfe *et al.*, in press), these parents may require special assistance in learning to remain calm as they attempt to ignore certain misbehaviors that previously elicited anger or frustration.

5.3.3.4. Learning to Ignore Misbehavior Is a Skill That Must Be Taught

Given that parents often have a long history of providing attention to misbehavior, and because they often experience emotional arousal or anger in difficult situations with their children, learning to ignore selectively certain child actions may require considerable practice and self-control by the parent. As Sulzer-Azaroff and Mayer (1977) have pointed out, the principle of ignoring misbehaviors is very easy to understand, but putting it into practice can be quite difficult. Beyond instruction in how to ignore certain types of misbehavior, the therapist may find it useful to rehearse with the parent how s/he will behave when the child engages in a targeted misbehavior, thereby allowing the parent to practice this skill. If the therapist makes home visits, or if child misbehavior occurs in the therapy setting (such as a waiting room, a playroom), modeling attention withdrawal for the parent to observe is also helpful. Finally, when the therapist observes parent–child interactions, feedback and instruction can be used to refine the parent's skill in using his or her attention to shape selectively child behavior.

Let us now briefly review several interventions where abusive parents were taught to ignore child misbehavior and to increase their attention to appropriate child actions. We will consider, in particular, the methods by which this form of parent training was accomplished.

5.4. REPRESENTATIVE RESEARCH ON TEACHING ABUSIVE PARENTS TO USE SELECTIVE ATTENTION

Most programs for training abusive parents to use appropriate child-management skills have included attention withdrawal as one component of a larger parenting treatment package (Crozier & Katz, 1979; Mastria *et al.*, 1979; Sandler *et al.*, 1978; Wolfe *et al.*, 1981c). In general, attention withdrawal is focused on child misbehaviors that frustrate the parent and elicit ineffective parental responses, while time out is usually reserved for the handling of more serious child behavior problems, especially those problems that are not being maintained by parent attention. All of these interventions also taught parents skills for positively reinforcing appropriate, desirable child behavior.

One of the most detailed reports of training a parent to use attention to modify selectively child behavior is the case study project by Wolfe *et al.* (1982). In this study, a 29-year-old mother was referred for treatment due to a history of handling her children's misbehavior through physical spankings and whippings. This disciplinary practice had resulted in injury to the children (welts, cuts, and bruises) on several occasions. The abused children were twin 9-year-old boys, and both were retarded. Parent interviews, caseworker reports, and direct observation of parent–child interactions in the clinic as well as the family's home indicated that the children engaged in a high rate of aversive, disruptive behavior (running about, throwing play objects at one another and at the parent, yelling to get the mother's attention) and noncompliance with parent requests. In her interactions with the children, the mother exhibited a very high rate of negative verbal attention when they misbehaved (e.g., "Tommy, stop doing that.,""Don't!," "You're making me mad"). Since the parent's physically violent responses (spanking or hitting) usually occurred when her efforts to control the children in this way were unsuccessful, intervention was directed toward teaching the parent to handle routine misbehavior more effectively.

In this project, a therapy team provided the parent with a rationale for selective attention as a child-management technique and outlined detailed guidelines for its use, similar to those presented earlier in this section. However, a major component of training was conducted in a clinic playroom, where the parent and children interacted during each session. In both assessment and training phases of the intervention, all family members engaged in structured, five-minute tasks intended to elicit cooperative, positive interactions (playing games together) and child noncompliance (where the parent made requests of the children to pick up and sort toys). Since child misbehavior occurred at a relatively high rate during these interactions, they provided an opportunity for the therapists to train directly the parent in the use of selective attention procedures.

In the Wolfe *et al.* (1982) study, a bug-in-the-ear (Stumphauzer, 1971) receiver was worn by the parent as she interacted with her children in the playroom. The therapist observed her interactions through a one-way mirror, and provided her with instructions over the device. For example, when one of the boys misbehaved or inappropriately attempted to get the parent's attention, the therapist instructed the parent to inhibit making any response and to ignore the child until the misbehavior ceased. Even when the child accelerated his rate of misbehavior in an effort to elicit a parental response, the therapist continued instruction to ignore these actions and to redirect positive attention (including praise and affectionate touching) when appropriate behavior occurred. If a highly disruptive or aggressive action took place (one child hit the other, threw a toy at the parent, or directly noncomplied with a parent request), the therapist provided instructions to the parent for implementing time out over the bug-in-the-ear device.

Figure 2 graphically presents an analysis of the parent's behavior during the cooperative and compliance interactions with her children. During baseline, the parent engaged in frequent hostile physical behaviors (raising her hand to threaten the child or grabbing the child) and hostile verbal comments when the children misbehaved. Positive comments or physical behaviors rarely occurred. With bug-in-the-ear training to ignore misbehavior, these attentional responses were almost entirely eliminated. Since the parent was coached to redirect positive attention when the child behaved appropriately, some increase in positive verbal and physical actions coincided with the reduction of attention to misbehavior. Midway through to intervention, the focus of training shifted to further strengthening the parent's skill in controlling her children's conduct through positive attention contingent on their good behavior; at that point, substantial increases in positive verbal and physical responses were evident.

As the parent in the Wolfe *et al.* (1982) study became proficient in

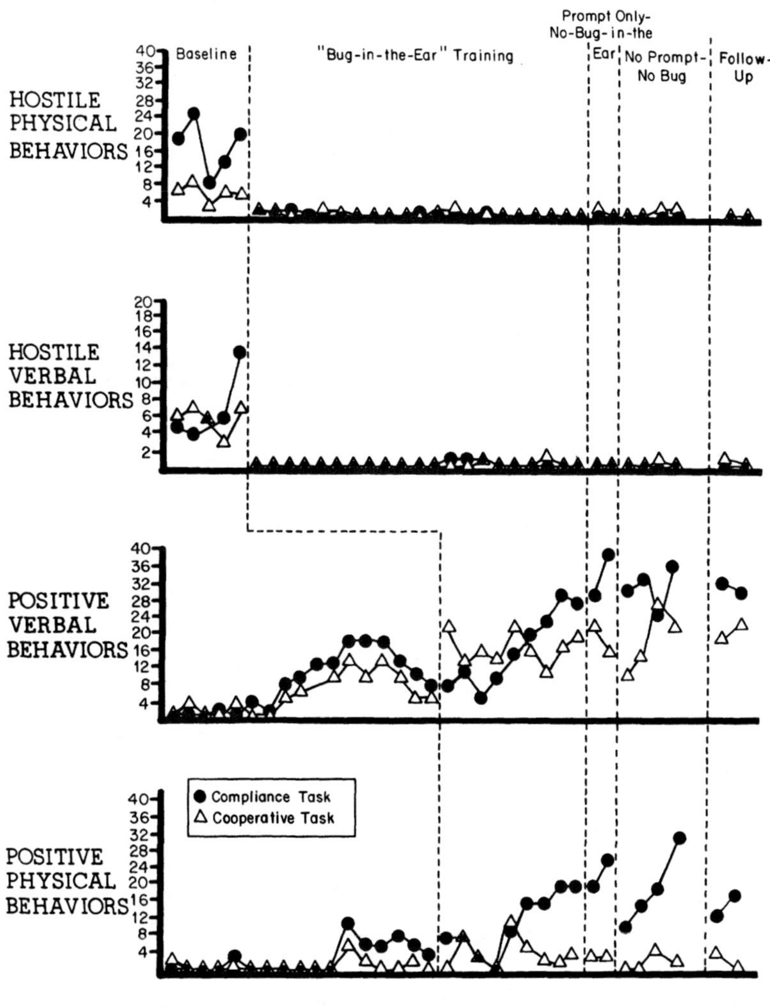

FIGURE 2. Rates of hostile and positive parent behavior toward children before and after training. [Reprinted from Wolfe, St. Lawrence, Graves, Brehony, Bradlyn, and Kelly (1982) with permission of the authors and *Behavior Therapy*. Copyright © 1982 the Association for Advancement of Behavior Therapy.]

withdrawing negative attention for child misbehavior and exhibiting positive attention for desirable behavior, use of the bug-in-the-ear device was faded. As Figure 2 shows, improvement was maintained when she was simply reminded once to use her skills, when no reminder was given, and at a follow-up conducted two months after the last bug-in-the-ear training session. In addition, periodic observations made in the home indicated that she used the skills appropriately in that setting as well.

This case application illustrates one way that therapists can directly teach a parent to ignore certain misbehaviors and provide attention for appropriate child actions the parent would like to see increase. Beyond instructing the parent how to handle the child, it was possible to observe directly parent–child behavior and shape the parent's conduct through coaching, modeling, rehearsal and reinforcement to the parent. Whenever possible, therapists should attempt to use these behavior change principles for teaching parents new child-management skills.

Finally, a case study reported by Scott *et al.* (1982) illustrates a treatment modification that proved useful when a parent was so angry with her child that she could not effectively ignore his misbehavior. In this family, the mother became extremely angry when her 10-year-old talked back, called her names, and was disruptive. On many occasions, she lost emotional control and hit the son; once the child was injured by a knife wound inflicted by the parent. While ignoring was felt by the authors to be an appropriate response when the child attempted to agitate the parent, the mother's own overarousal in these situations was such that she would experience difficulty withdrawing attention. Therefore, treatment first focused on teaching the parent anger-control techniques including cognitive-modification skills to foster self-calming and relaxation skills to reduce cues of physiological arousal. After the mother mastered better anger-control strategies, she then received comprehensive and successful training in the use of selective attention. The successful combination of child-management and anger-coping training have also been reported by other investigators (Denicola & Sandler, 1980).

In this chapter, we have discussed several techniques that abusive parents can be taught in order to help them control child misbehavior without resorting to excessive violence or physical punitiveness. For parents who experience difficulty handling their children's behavior problems nonviolently, training in this area may be a priority for intervention. However, a related and equally important goal is helping parents to use positive reinforcement-based practices with their children. We will now turn our attention to this aspect of child-management training.

6

Teaching Parents to Use Positive Reinforcement Skills

While teaching abusive parents nonviolent methods to control child misbehavior is often an immediate, necessary aim of child-management training, it is rarely a sufficient form of family intervention. Simply stated, therapists should never train parents to use attention withdrawal or time out procedures without concurrently teaching them how to reinforce desirable child behavior. Extinction-based management techniques are most effective when a child learns not only that certain misbehaviors will not result in reinforcement, but also that other desirable actions will be noticed and responded to in a positive way. In addition, since abusive parents provide less verbal attention to their children than nonabusive parents (Burgess & Conger, 1978), it might well be considered unfair or unethical to instruct them simply to reduce further the amount of attention given to their youngsters. Therefore, a clinical aim is to assist parents in altering and redirecting the attention they provide, from negative notice contingent upon child misbehavior to demonstrative positive reinforcement contingent upon appropriate child behavior.

There is another more global rationale for encouraging abusive parents to use positive-based techniques with their children. Clinical and research descriptions of child-abusive parents indicate that these individuals often have negative feelings toward their children, may expect that their youngsters will cause them difficulty, and find it difficult to identify positive child attributes and behavior (Blumberg, 1974; Friedrich & Boriskin, 1976; Green, 1976). If parents have a history of few positive interactions with their children and experience difficulty handling child behavior problems, the development of such negative cognitions and feelings would be anticipated. Further, from a cognitive-dissonance perspective (Festinger, 1957), some parents may perceive their children as being "mean," "uncontrollable," or "deserving of punishment" in order to create cognitive consistency and thereby justify the harsh conduct they feel is necessary to impose.

For all of these reasons, therapists should carefully develop interventions that improve the quality of parent–child interactions in abusive families by teaching parents to use effectively positive-reinforcement techniques. Not only will such intervention further broaden the parent's child-management skills repertoire, but it can also interrupt a cycle in which parents observe, perceive, and respond primarily to their children's aversive behavior.

In this chapter we will discuss parent training of two types: (1) using social reinforcement and attention to strengthen desirable child behavior and (2) teaching parents to develop structured contingency-management techniques to reduce problems such as noncompliance.

6.1. TRAINING PARENTS TO USE ATTENTION TO REINFORCE DESIRABLE BEHAVIOR

Clinicians and researchers have long observed that parents are likely to notice and provide attentional recognition for children's misbehavior, but allow appropriate actions to go unnoticed and ignored. As we saw in the last chapter, parents can become more effective managers of their children's behavior if they remove reinforcement for inappropriate conduct and provide increased reinforcement contingent upon appropriate child behavior. Unfortunately, just as "ignore misbehavior" is a direction that is easy to give but difficult for parents to actually follow, vague therapist directives to "praise more" are also likely to be ineffective. Instead, a careful intervention plan should be developed in which (1) specific child behaviors are identified and targeted for treatment; (2) principles of social reinforcement are fully taught to the parent; (3) the parent's skill in using these techniques is assessed; and (4) change in the child's behavior is evaluated following intervention. Let us review each of these areas.

6.1.1. Identifying Child Behaviors for Intervention

Since reinforcement techniques function to increase the frequency of behavior, they are ordinarily targeted for actions that one would like to see occur more often. The selection of specific target behaviors for intervention depends on the results of a family's assessment. Parent interview descriptions of problem situations, behavior problem checklists, and the results of therapist observation of parent–child interactions can all provide useful information on situations where the parent is currently failing to provide sufficient reinforcement to promote desired child behavior. In the Wolfe *et al.* (1981c) project, parents were asked to record any child-management problems that took place between weekly home visits by their therapist; the parents then received training in how to handle each identified problem using positive techniques when the therapist made home visits. In the treatment reports by Mastria *et al.* (1979), Crimmins *et al.* (1982), and Wolfe *et al.* (1982), therapists observed interactions between abusive parents and their children, and assessed how frequently parents directed positive attention (reinforcing verbal comments, affectionate touches, and similar components of attention) when the children behaved appropriately (e.g., by following a parent's direction or playing cooperatively). Since the abusive parents in these studies rarely directed any positive social attention to their children, training in positive-reinforcement skills was deemed necessary.

Table 3 lists a number of specific child behaviors that have been targeted in treatment studies where parents were taught to use social reinforcement more effectively. Inspection of this list shows that attention can be used both to increase some desired behavior that occurs too infrequently at present, or to decrease an undesirable behavior (such as running about a room) by reinforcing an action that is

TABLE 3
Several Child Behavior Problems Successfully Treated Using Contingent Attention and Attention Removal Techniques

Target behavior	Child age	Intervention	Source
Aggression	3 and 4	Attention reinforcement for periods of cooperative behavior, with time out for instances of aggression	Lavigueur, Peterson, Sheese, & Peterson, 1973; Zeilberger, Sampen, & Sloane, 1968
Fighting between siblings	16 children, mean age = 6	Contingent attention reinforcement when children interacted appropriately	Leitenberg, Burchard, Burchard, Fuller, & Lysaght, 1977
"Hyperactivity" at mealtimes	3	Contingent attention for appropriate behavior, with time out for misbehavior	Frazier & Schneider, 1975
Noncompliance	27 mother–child dyads	Praise for complying with parent requests; time out for noncompliance	Roberts, McMahon, Forehand, & Humphreys, 1978; Wahler, 1969
Whining and shouting	4	Nonattention to the misbehavior, attention contingent on appropriate behavior	Hall, Axelrod, Tyler, Grief, Jones, & Robertson, 1972
Tantrums	9	Nonattention for tantrum behavior, attention for appropriate behavior, with instruction by mother in self-control techniques	Strober & Bellack, 1975

incompatible with the undesired behavior (e.g., providing attention and praise when the child plays more quietly with a game). In either case, parent attention is used selectively and contingently to increase the child's frequency of appropriate behavior.

Following discussion with a parent, the therapist can pinpoint an appropriate target behavior for intervention. If time out or attention withdrawal is being planned, concurrent intervention to reinforce a desirable action incompatible with the misbehavior is often logical. For example, if a parent will use time out to handle her child's tantrums, a program can be simultaneously implemented to reinforce occasions when the child plays appropriately and does not tantrum. In order to maximize the likelihood that training will be successful and that the parent will learn that positive attention is a potent management technique, it is desirable to focus attention on a single or a very limited number of problem situations at one time. By doing so, the therapist will be better able to monitor specific change in the child's behavior and to assess whether the parent is actually implementing reinforcement skills in the targeted situation correctly.

6.1.2. Teaching Parents to Use Praise and Positive Attention Correctly

Behavior-management programs are most effective when the person implementing them—in this case, the parent—understands the major learning principles upon which reinforcement programs are based. Even praise and attention, which appear to be very uncomplicated skills, will be more successfully used if the following principles are reviewed with parents.

6.1.2.1. Immediacy

All forms of reinforcement, including praise and attention, are most potent when they closely follow the actions that the parent seeks to encourage. This is particularly true for children, whose behavior is likely to be unaffected by reinforcing consequences that are delayed. Thus, if a parent wants to reinforce a child's compliance with his or her requests, praise and attention should be given *while* the child is following the parent's direction and not at some point later in the day.

6.1.2.2. Verbal Labeling and Specificity of Praise

Verbal reinforcement is most effective when a parent not only commends the child's behavior, but also communicates what specific action of the child is being noticed (cf. Bernhardt & Forehand, 1975; Kelly, 1983). For example, "It's good when you play with your game without throwing it" conveys more specific information to the youngster than a simple "That's good." Presumably, receiving labeled praise helps children to better discriminate among those actions that will elicit favorable reactions from their parents (Sulzer-Azaroff & Mayer, 1977). Further, the verbal linking of praise to a specific child action may provide a stronger basis for later self-control and self-statement-guided behavior by the child (Aronfreed, 1968).

6.1.2.3. Frequency

Extensive research on the delivery of reinforcement clearly indicates that frequent reinforcement leads to the most rapid, effective acquisition of new behavior (Miller, 1980; Rettig, 1973). Consequently, when a parent is first attempting to increase a child's appropriate behavior, the desired action should be praised and should receive attention every time it is observed to occur. For temporally ongoing behaviors (such as playing appropriately with a game over an extended period or interacting with a sibling without fighting), positive attention can be provided at frequent intervals as the child continues to behave well. Later, after clear improvement in the child's conduct is evident, intermittent or occasional attention contingent upon appropriate behavior is often sufficient to maintain it.

6.1.2.4. Diversity or Novelty of Reinforcement

Repetitive forms of verbal praise may lose their novelty and cease functioning as reinforcing events for a child. Frequent repetitions of "That's good . . . "That's good . . . That's good" can easily lose reinforcement value and, with it, their ability to influence behavior. It is helpful to teach parents to develop and use a range of different verbal comments to communicate praise so that boredom and satiation effects do not become problematic. Further, training to include physically warm aspects of attention (eye contact, smiling, hugs, affectionate touching) may also be needed. In a study by Wolfe *et al.* (1982), an abusive parent was taught to use a number of different verbal praise comments to combine occasionally or vary them with physically affectionate gestures when the child behaved appropriately.

6.1.2.5. Demonstrativeness of Attention

For attention to modify effectively a child's behavior, the youngster must be aware that the parent did observe his or her conduct and that the parent was pleased. This requires parents to acquire the skill of conveying positive feelings, comments, and attention in a warm, demonstrative manner; mumbled praise and unconvincing affect are likely to carry little reinforcement value for most children. In the context of adult social skills, Lazarus (1971) has pointed out that many people have well-developed competencies for criticizing others and conveying anger, but are seriously deficient in situations where they must communicate positive feelings and affection. In analogous fashion, parents accustomed to negative interactions with their children may encounter difficulty genuinely exhibiting positive forms of attention. Specific training in this area is often needed.

6.1.3. Training Parents to Use Positive Attention

Discussion and instruction to parents are generally the first steps for teaching parents to use their positive attention as a child-management technique. With abusive parents who are seriously skills-deficient, more active and practice-based training is also necessary. Several different training procedures have been used in interventions with child-abusive parents.

Crozier and Katz (1979) describe a training procedure that utilizes reading and discussion of child-management techniques, followed by therapist modeling and behavior rehearsal of the same management skills. In the modeling–rehearsal component of training sessions, the parent first plays the role of the child while the therapist demonstrates correct uses and examples of the skill. Later, the therapist assumes the role of the child while the parent practices appropriately using the trained skill. During sessions, the therapist provides feedback, further modeling, and praise as the parent correctly exhibits new skills.

This form of in-session modeling-rehearsal is desirable because it permits the therapist to demonstrate key elements for using attention effectively, including the modeling of a variety of verbal praise comments, nonverbal aspects of positive attention, and optimal style and demonstrativeness of praise. Since the parent then rehearses the same skills, a behavioral measure of parent performance can be obtained and evaluated. The major limitation of this training technique is that, if it is used alone, the therapist does not observe how adequately the parent applies the same skill with his or her child. However, additional assessment and training during actual parent–child interactions can easily be incorporated into an intervention following parent–therapist rehearsal training sessions.

Studies by Sandler and his associates (Denicola & Sandler, 1980; Sandler *et al.*, 1978; Wolfe & Sandler, 1981; Wolfe *et al.*, 1981c) have all made use of in-the-home assessment and training procedures, often in conjunction with other parent-training sessions that took place in a clinic setting. In the Wolfe and Sandler (1981) project, parents were first presented with reading materials and sample behavior problem situations to help them acquire knowledge of proper child-management skills. Then, the therapist interacted with the parent's child and modeled appropriate use of the skills while the parent observed. Finally, the parent and child interacted with one another, with the parent instructed to practice using the skill behavior that was receiving attention in that day's training. Since the therapist was present and directly observed the interaction, additional feedback, praise, and suggestions could be provided to the parent. Direct training of this type can be provided when parent–child interactions are "staged" in a clinic playroom setting, although it is probably even more effective to conduct some training sessions in the home since that is the critical environment where change must ultimately take place.

A slightly different procedure for teaching abusive parents to use positive attention involves bug-in-the-ear training (Stumphauzer, 1971). Described in the previous chapter, this device enables the therapist to offer coaching and instruction to shape more effective skills while the parent is engaging in interactions with his or her child. A desirable feature of "bug-based" training is that it permits the therapist to provide feedback and suggestions during the actual course of an ongoing interaction, rather than following the interaction. One disadvantage, however, is the device's rather high cost. While applications of bug-in-the-ear training with abusive families have been conducted in clinic settings (e.g., as parents and children interact in a playroom; Crimmins *et al.*, 1982; Wolfe *et al.*, 1982), therapists can certainly develop an expanded treatment that also includes observation and parent training in the home environment.

To summarize, treatment intended to shape a parent's skill in using positive-attention controls to increase appropriate child behavior will ideally include several training components. These are:

1. *Information on how to use attention effectively*, provided verbally by the therapist and accompanied by written instructional materials.
2. *Modeling of appropriate skill use by the therapist*, either during behavior rehearsal session between the therapist and the parent (cf. Crozier & Katz, 1979) or, preferably, with the parent observing as the therapist interacts with his/her child and models correct skills (cf. Wolfe & Sandler, 1981).
3. *Parent practice in using the skill* with the therapist present and observing the interaction in order to assess the parent's skill and to provide feedback, reinforcement, or corrective instruction. While this practice can take place during staged parent–child interactions in the clinic setting, it is extremely desirable to conduct home visits so the therapist can observe and train skills in this setting as well.
4. *Identifying a limited number of current problem situations and instructing the parent to use positive attention skills systematically;* targeted situations might include management problems similar to those listed in Table 3, or other difficulties where increased reinforcement of desirable child behavior would reduce family conflict.
5. *Assessing the impact of training*. This can include a direct observational assessment of how frequently or how effectively the parent exhibits positive attention skills during staged interactions with the child in a playroom (cf. Mastria *et al.*, 1979; Wolfe *et al.*, 1982) or, more importantly, in the family's own

home (cf. Crozier & Katz, 1979; Denicola & Sandler, 1980; Sandler *et al.*, 1978). In addition, when intervention is focused on a limited number of problem situations, parents can be asked to monitor the child's behavior and their own conduct in those situations; this can yield important clinical data on whether child-management skills training is having its desired effect. With this assessment procedure, Scott *et al.* (1982) were able to demonstrate increases in an abusive mother's self-monitored frequency of praise and decreases in her child's rate of misbehavior following intervention.

Teaching parents to use positive attention to promote desirable behavior is a potent child-management intervention. When parents become proficient in selectively reinforcing appropriate behavior and removing attention for misbehavior, they can be encouraged to apply the skill to a wide range of problem situations that occur in many different settings. Because the behavior of even very young children is influenced by its attentional consequences, parent training in this technique is clinically relevant for a large number of families. However, other methods for systematically reinforcing appropriate child behavior can be incorporated within treatment programs for abusive parents. We will next consider training abusive parents to use other reinforcement-based contingency-management techniques.

6.2. IN-THE-HOME CONTINGENCY-MANAGEMENT PROGRAMS

Praise and attention are social reinforcers since they occur in the context of the interpersonal relationship between the parent and child. However, nonsocial events of many kinds can also function as reinforcers and can be used to alter and manage the behavior of children. The term "contingency management" refers to a process in which parents use the principles of reinforcement to increase a child's desirable conduct at home. While the correct use of praise and attention involve contingency-management skills, in this section we will focus primarily on child-management programs that utilize nonsocial (or *tangible*) reinforcers.

Just as parents apply attention and attention withdrawal techniques to specific target misbehaviors of their children, implementing a structured contingency-management program also requires the clear identification of specific child behaviors to be targeted for change. Four criteria can be used to select behaviors included in a reinforcement-based contingency-management system. First, the target behavior should be *definable in a clear, objective manner* that can be understood by both the parent and the child. "Being good," "listening," or "being cooperative" are inappropriate choices as target behavior because they are overly ambiguous. "Putting toys in the closet," "Being dressed for school by 7:30," or "Taking a bath after only one reminder" are more clearly defined and, therefore, are better targets for intervention. A second criterion is that the behaviors targeted for intervention should be *positive, appropriate actions that a parent would like to see occur more often.* Since reinforcement is a response-increasing strategy, it should be focused on desirable actions the parent wants to promote. These might be good behaviors that now occur infrequently, actions that presently occur only after repeated parental nagging or threatening, or desirable behavior that is incompatible with some misbehavior the parent wants to reduce. Third, reinforcement programs should only target *behaviors that the child is capable of exhibiting.* Complex skills that are not yet in a youngster's repertoire (such as correct initial toilet use, new study skills, or overcoming fears) often require intensive shaping that ordinary contingency-management programs do not provide.

A final and clinically important criterion when working with child-abusive parents is to focus on *target behaviors that will reduce the potential for family violence.* In the study reported by Wolfe *et al.* (1981b), an abusive parent beat her children when they dawdled excessively getting ready for school in the morning. The target behavior selected for intervention in this case was increasing the child's willingness to prepare for school, since learning to handle this problem appropriately would reduce the parent's likelihood of violence. In the intervention, a program to reinforce the child's "ready-for-school-on-time" behavior was successfully implemented and there were not further incidents of violence. The important point here is that training will have its maximum clinical impact when a parent learns to handle, in a positive manner, those behavior problems that previously elicited frustration, anger, or violence. This highlights the importance of a careful pretreatment family assessment that provides information on the specific management problems which will require attention.

6.2.1. Selection of Reinforcers

When the therapist and parent have together targeted behaviors for intervention, the next task is determining what reinforcers will be used in the behavior change program. A comprehensive discussion of the properties of positive reinforcement with children is beyond the scope of this book, and readers unfamiliar with this topic may wish to consult a more detailed source (see, for example, Forehand & McMahon, 1981; Miller, 1980; Rimm & Masters, 1979; or Sulzer-Azaroff & Mayer, 1977). However, a therapist can survey with the parent/s and child possible tangible and activity reinforcers that can be made contingent upon the child's appropriate behavior. Examples of possible tangible reinforcers include favorite food items or access to special toys, dolls, games, puzzles, or coloring books. Examples of activity reinforcers include television-watching time, special game periods with the parent, the opportunity to stay up shortly past one's usual bedtime, listening to children's records, or having a special story read by the parent. Reinforcers are not absolutes; an event that is reinforcing to one child might have little reward value to another. The important task is identifying those reinforcers that are functional for the treated family's child.

As the therapist assesses potential reinforcers that can be used in a family's intervention, several practical matters should be considered:

Can the reinforcer be made contingent on the child's behavior? If a youngster watches television on an unlimited, noncontingent basis, a special television-watching period following good behavior is unlikely to have much impact. Instead, a highly reinforcing activity or event that can be made to depend on the child's good behavior should be sought. To be effective, a reinforcer must not only have value or importance to a child, but must also be available only when the child engages in the desired target behavior.

Will the parent be able to provide the reinforcer consistently and over an extended period of time? Let's suppose that a major source of conflict in one family is their six-year-old's unwillingness to take a bath. Problems at bath time lead to frustration, anger, and even spanking of the youngster. In a program to encourage child compliance, the parents might offer the child a puzzle or game contingent on taking a nightly bath with only one reminder. If the youngster enjoys puzzles and does not have unlimited access to them presently, this could be the basis of an effective contingency-management program. However, will the parents actually be willing or able to buy a different puzzle each day for the child? Rather than develop a program which proves difficult because the selected reinforcers cannot be provided appropriately, practical alternatives should be explored. In this example, the parents could purchase several puzzles, and allow their child to pick one for a special play period after his bath. This approach can be made part of the family's daily routine, whereas the new-puzzle-every-day plan would be difficult for most families to maintain.

Reinforcers with low potential for satiation are desirable or a variety of different reinforcers should be made available. We have already alluded to the notion of "reinforcement value," a term that refers to the potency or strength of a reinforcer (Rotter, 1954). Presumably, events with high-reinforcement value to a child will more strongly increase and maintain behavior than those with low value or potency. If a child has a strong preference for watching television, but spends little time playing with puzzles, television-watching has the higher reinforcement value and is therefore a better consequence for use in a behavior-management program.

Children, like adults, sometimes satiate or lose interest in the same reinforcer over time; an event that was a reinforcer for behavior can cease to function as one if the child satiates of it. This problem can be minimized by incorporating into contingency-management programs reinforcers that have high initial reinforcement value to the child, are relatively novel, and are attainable primarily through good behavior performance, rather than being commonly available. It is also possible to offer the child one of several different reinforcers (sometimes termed a reinforcement "menu") contingent upon his/her good behavior; when the six-year-old in our previous example takes a bath without repeated nagging or threatening, he might be given a choice of playing with a puzzle, having a special bedtime story read to him, or staying up 15 minutes later than usual. In this way, the diversity of events would help to reduce the possibility that the child will become satiated and bored with the program.

Delivery of reinforcement should closely follow the desired child behavior. Any reinforcer used in a contingency-management program should be one that can be delivered closely following the child's exhibition of the desired behavior. Delayed reinforcement is much less effective than immediate reinforcement, and it is preferable to utilize small, manageable reinforcers that can be provided quickly than to offer "major" rewards (a trip to the zoo or a new tricycle) that must be delayed or are infrequently available.

After the therapist and parent have targeted a problem and decided upon suitable reinforcers for the contingency-management program, it is possible to develop an actual intervention plan. To illustrate how this can be accomplished, we will review one case example and then consider several characteristics of all effective management programs.

6.2.2. Implementing an At-Home Contingency-Management System: A Case Example

Five-year-old Tommy was described by his mother as a noncompliant child who ignored directions and frustrated the parent. While the parent's usual response to such child misbehavior involved repeating requests and nagging, on some occasions she would become more angry and physically punitive. The family came to the attention of child welfare authorities when, during a spanking episode, the son fell against a table and sustained a gash on the head. It appeared that this parent lacked the child-management skills needed to handle child behavior problems effectively.

Initial assessment consisted of parent interviews, completion of a behavior problem checklist to identify problematic management situations, monitoring of child-management problems over a one-week period, and an at-home session to observe directly parent–child interactions. Based on these sources of data, it was possible to identify specific situations where Tommy's noncompliant behavior caused the mother difficulty. One problem that occurred almost every night during the monitoring week was the child's refusal to pick up his toys before going to bed. Every evening, Tommy pulled out many toys and playthings, but rarely put them back in the drawer after he was finished. When his mother asked him to put things away, Tommy either ignored her request or defiantly refused to do it. This, in turn, precipitated a series of reminders, angry threats and, on occasion, physical discipline by the mother. While Tommy's mother seemed to understand that failure to pick up toys was not in itself a major or dramatic behavior problem, she felt angry that the child would purposefully disregard her directions.

For one week, the parent simply monitored the child's behavior and recorded how often he picked up his toys with just one reminder from the mother. He never did. Then, an intervention was started. Interviews with the parent, corrobrated by Tommy himself, indicated that the child liked to have bedtime stories read to him by his mother; at present, she read stories to Tommy, but not on a consistent or regular schedule. A contingency-management program was initiated in which Tommy would need to put away all of his toys with just one reminder from the parent by 7:45, about 15 minutes before his bedtime. Mother was instructed to give the single prompt at about 7:30. If Tommy picked up his toys and put them in the agreed upon storage places, the parent immediately praised this behavior and let Tommy select the story she would read to him that night at bedtime. If he was noncompliant and did not follow her one request, Tommy went immediately to bed without a story. On any unsuccessful nights, the parents was instructed to refrain from visibly showing she was angry or upset, but to matter-of-factly tell Tommy she would not read to him that night because of his noncompliant behavior.

In this example, a rather simple contingency or relationship was established between a child's behavior the parent sought to encourage (picking up toys) and a reinforcer the child would work to obtain (a special story-reading time). By focusing on a problem area where child noncompliance had been problematic, the program also would reduce noncompliant behavior and, consequently, lessen the likelihood of conflict between the parent and child. More important, the parent here learned a strategy for improving her child's behavior through positive reinforcement techniques, rather than by using threats or punitive responses.

There are several practical matters for therapists to consider when training parents to use contingency-management techniques at home. Often, the failure of a program to function successfully is due to problems in one or more of these areas. Let's consider several key points.

1. *A behavior targeted for change must be defined specifically and be understood by both the parent and the child.* Earlier, we noted that target behaviors should be behaviorally specific ("picking up toys from the floor when asked") rather than global and imprecise ("listening to me"). It is sometimes necessary to "tie" the performance of the desired behavior to a certain time of day, as was the case in this example, or to clarify what is meant by a certain behavior. An action such as "getting ready for bed" requires definition because the parent and child may have different ideas about what behavior constitutes getting ready for bed.

2. *Guidelines for how to prompt a desired child behavior should be included in parent training.* Usually, one reminder is given to the child by the parent in order to prompt a desired behavior; if repeated requests are made, the program will not reduce parent nagging and frustration. Repeated reminders also convey to the child that the first prompt can be ignored. When reviewing this with parents, the therapist may wish to model and role play with the parent how to make appropriate, effective requests of children; this practice ensures that the parent learns to communicate commands or directions in a clear, specific, and informative manner to the child.

3. *The positive reinforcers used in the system should be sufficiently potent to increase the child's behavior.* Any effort to define a reinforcer for a child must be regarded as a tentative hypothesis until it is shown to be effective in changing the child's behavior. Thus, although it appeared that a bedtime story would be reinforcing for Tommy, if his behavior did *not* change when he could have a story read to him, the

selection of this as an effective reinforcer would have been incorrect. In that event, the therapist should reevaluate the program and attempt to identify and use other more potent types of reinforcers. In related fashion, it is important to ensure that access to a reinforcer is contingent upon the child's good behavior. If Tommy's mother read stories to him every night even if he did not pick up his toys, this reinforcer would probably be ineffective for his behavior change program.

4. *Contingency-management efforts should be kept as uncomplicated as possible.* This author has seen families where such elaborate rules, programs, and multiple contingencies were simultaneously implemented that no one in the family, including the parent, could easily describe how the system worked. Under such circumstances, consistency is difficult to achieve. In general, it appears preferable to focus on just one or two problem behaviors at a time in a structured contingency-management program.

5. *Praise and positive social attention always accompany the delivery of any tangible or activity reinforcers.* Earlier in this chapter, the role of attentional reinforcement was discussed in detail. Contingency-management programs should always incorporate parent praise in addition to the provision of tangible reinforcers. When the child engages in a desired behavior, the first response of the parent is to praise and recognize the child's actions; the delivery of tangible or special activities can be considered as added "backups" that provide still further attention and recognition of the child's accomplishment. They do not, however, replace the more personal and important role of parent praise.

6. *When parents implement a contingency-management program of any kind, data on its effectiveness should be obtained and reviewed with the therapist.* Parents can monitor the frequency of a specific behavior problem before and following the implementation of a reinforcement program, with this information reviewed and discussed during therapy sessions. Beyond changes in the child's behavior, it is also useful to review periodically with a parent how an already-implemented

program is functioning, whether it is being consistently followed, and whether the program is, in fact, reducing conflicts between the parent and child.

As we have seen in the past two chapters, child-management training for abusive parents entails instruction and behavioral practice in a number of different competencies. Teaching parents to use nonviolent alternatives instead of physical punishment, to use attention to increase desirable behavior or decrease child misbehavior, and to apply affective contingency-management skills for handling specific behavior problems can be helpful in cases where child-directed violence occurs because parents lack the skills to manage child behavior nonviolently. While all instances of abuse do not stem from child-management skill deficits, direct training in these techniques is appropriate and necessary for many families.

7

Anger-Control Training for Abusive Parents

Earlier, when a social-learning conceptualization of child abuse was first described, we noted that parent anger is often an immediate antecedent to a child-abusive act. With the unusual exception of parents who calmly, intentionally seek to injure their children, or those who exhibit violent behavior so frequently that it becomes an acceptable and unemotional response, most abusive parents inflict injuries at times when they are angry (Statistical Report on Child Abuse and Neglect in Hawaii, 1975). Impulsive anger has been a personality characteristic widely observed in clinical reports of abusive parents (Green, 1976; Kempe, 1973; Kempe *et al.*, 1962; Steele & Pollock, 1968). More recently, controlled studies have demonstrated that abusive parents exhibit atypical, heightened physiological arousal and self-reported anger when presented with realistic cues of aversive child behavior (Disbrow *et al.*, 1977; Frodi & Lamb, 1980; Wolfe *et al.*, in press). Taken together, all of these findings suggest that anger arousal accompanies many instances of child abuse and, therefore, that the likelihood of violent behavior in such families should be reduced if the parent develops appropriate means to handle anger more effectively. This is particularly true if the parent's current high-probability response when angry is physical aggression directed toward the child.

Before one can intervene to reduce a parent's likelihood for exhibiting child-directed violence when angry, it is important to consider carefully what specific stimuli, situations, or other factors actually elicit anger. In the chapter on assessment, we noted that a variety of different events can serve to evoke anger, including arousal to *aversive cues* emitted by the child (such as crying or screaming), intensified anger resulting from unsuccessful attempts to handle a difficult *management situation*, or frustration and anger elicited by *some event other than the child*. An example of the latter is a parent who encounters frustration in relationships or owing to economic stress and, when experiencing this heightened degree of emotional arousal, is more apt to respond aggressively toward his or her child.

The source or the stimuli which elicit anger determine the type of intervention that is needed to help parents cope with it. For example, if a parent experiences anger arousal when his or her child simply emits an aversive cue such as crying, a desensitization procedure that teaches the parent to use relaxation and self-calming skills in the presence of those cues may be an adequate anger-control intervention. On the other hand, if a parent experiences arousal when s/he is unable to handle a child's repeated misbehavior, anger-control training alone is probably an insufficient treatment; here, the parent would need to learn effective child-management skills *and* acquire techniques for self-calming in the troublesome situation. In similar fashion, frustration which stems from some difficulty outside the parent–child relationship (such as marital discord, joblessness, or financial problems) may well require attention to both reducing the external stress *and* helping the parent learn to cope more effectively with feelings of anger or frustration. For these reasons, anger-control treatment for abusive parents is ordinarily combined with some other training in the specific competencies that are needed to actually handle the difficult situation more skillfully. To date, anger-control intervention has most often been combined with child-management skills training (Crozier & Katz, 1979; Denicola & Sandler, 1980; Mastria *et al.*, 1979; Wolfe *et al.*, 1981c). The aim of this combination treatment is to help the parent control anger, avoid making an immediate aggressive response in a difficult child-management situation, and instead implement an appropriate, nonviolent solution to the problem.

7.1. PROGRESSING FROM ASSESSMENT DATA TO AN ANGER-CONTROL INTERVENTION PLAN

As we outlined in Chapter 4, an abusive parent's anger problems are evaluated by means of information obtained in *interviews* (assessing whether violent episodes occur when the parent is feeling anger, what specific events elicit anger, how frequently anger is experienced, how the parent now reports handling anger) and daily self-monitoring logs in which the parent records any episodes of anger along with their antecedents and consequences. Occasionally, physiological assessment of arousal when the parent is presented with cues of aversive child behavior or anger self-report inventories (such as the Novaco Anger Scale; Novaco, 1975) are also used as assessment and treatment-planning instruments.

7.1.1. Development of an Anger Situations Hierarchy

The therapist's careful review of all these assessment data is likely to reveal a number of different situations that elicit varying degrees of anger response by the parent. For example, in one family, a child's crying and whining may result in reactions of only mild irritation by the parent, while extended tantrumming and noncompliance elicit greater anger, and acts of destructiveness or name-calling toward the parent result in extreme anger and loss of emotional control. The likelihood of a violent, aggressive response toward the child can itself vary based on the strength of anger, as well as other factors, including the parent's typical way of responding to that aversive child behavior and the parent's labeling of the child's intentions. It is possible, therefore, to develop a graded hierarchy of situations where the parent currently experiences anger, from situations which elicit only mild arousal and carry little likelihood of aggression, to those where the parent feels emotionally out of control and where violence is much more likely to take place. The number of problem situations included in this hierarchy depends, of course, on the range of situations that have evoked anger and/or been associated with child-directed violence; Novaco (1978) has suggested that approximately seven scenes be included in a typical anger hierarchy. Each situation should be recorded in sufficient detail for the therapist to later recount it fully to the parent.

The careful development of a hierarchy or graded list of situations that evoke progressively greater amounts of anger is the initial step for anger-control intervention (Dubanowski *et al.*, 1978; Novaco, 1978). These scenes are used for basic rehearsal and desensitization training purposes during clinic visits, and early homework practice assignments involve applying anger-control skills to cope with the corresponding in vivo situations more effectively. Later, training is broadened to encompass additional, novel anger-producing situations that the parent may encounter. We will turn now to the treatment elements which comprise anger-control intervention.

7.2. COMPONENTS OF ANGER-CONTROL TRAINING

Like many complex psychological phenomena, anger is the product of several different but interrelated response modalities, including heightened *physiological arousal, cognitions or labeling processes* in which one generates self-statements that serve to produce or maintain anger, and *behavioral responses* (such as shouting, pacing, or hitting) that are the results of anger and often also function as cues to maintain continued anger (Lazarus, 1966; Novaco, 1978). Since anger is characterized by responses in several modalities, intervention to control it generally combines attention to reducing the person's physiological arousal (through relaxation techniques), anger-related cognitions (by cognitive modification), and overt anger behaviors (by teaching alternative responses in the difficult situation). In the next sections, anger-control treatment procedures will be described in detail and their specific applications for child-abusive parents will be discussed.

7.2.1. Relaxation Training

Relaxation training is one of the most venerable, widely used, and widely studied techniques in the history of behavior therapy.

With detailed procedures for deep muscle relaxation appearing as early as the 1930s (Jacobsen, 1938), relaxation training has been successfully incorporated into treatments for anxiety and phobias, stress-related difficulties, and a wide range of psychophysiological disorders (see reviews by Blanchard & Ahles, 1979; Borkovec & Sides, 1979; Hillenberg & Collins, 1982). Wolpe (1958), theorizing that arousal and physiological relaxation are incompatible biological "opposites," provided a rationale for the use of relaxation in systematic desensitization. In desensitization, persons are systematically taught to relax in the presence of stimuli that elicit anxiety or arousal; over repeated practice experiences, arousal to those stimuli is expected to weaken as the classically conditioned "link" between the stimulus and the former anxiety response is extinguished (Wolpe, 1958, 1973). From a somewhat different perspective, teaching persons to relax deeply when confronted by arousing cues provides them with a new self-control response option for handling situations that formerly led to anxious, angry, and perhaps violent behavior.

In the specific case of child-abusive behavior, we can hypothesize that if a parent is taught to relax in situations that previously elicited anger, a number of desirable consequences will follow. First, the parent will learn to handle an unpleasant mood state better and be less likely to feel "out-of-control" in difficult situations. Second, and related to the first point, the effects of self-calming are likely to permit the parent to evaluate more fully and effectively how best to deal with a problematic situation. High levels of anxiety are known to disrupt performance in complex tasks (Yerkes & Dodson, 1908), and extremely high levels of anger arousal in a situation may also inhibit an individual's effective problem-solving. Thus, the angry parent's response to a child misbehavior might be an impulsive strike, while the same parent, if calm, would be better able to arrive at a nonviolent solution to the problem.

Training parents to use relaxation techniques involves several treatment steps. These are initial teaching and practice in basic self-relaxation skills, followed by *assignments* to apply relaxation techniques in the actual situations that presently elicit anger. Anger-control intervention may also include *in-clinic* desensitization procedures as an intermediate step between skills training and *in vivo* application (Novaco, 1975, 1976, 1978).

7.2.1.1. *Training Basic Relaxation Skills*

Initial relaxation practice usually takes place in the clinic or office setting and is intended to help an individual master basic self-relaxation skills. While there are a number of different relaxation-training techniques, most focus on inducing deep muscle relaxation followed by relaxing cognitive imagery of some kind.

Therapists inexperienced with relaxation-training procedures should consult a specialized source for detailed information on the use of this technique, such as Bernstein and Borkovec (1973), Goldfried and Davison (1976), or Jacobsen (1970). Each contains excellent and specific suggestions for the conduct of relaxation-training sessions. The major components of treatment include the following:

1. A rationale for relaxation training is provided to the client. This rationale includes a statement that effective, deep relaxation is a skill that must be learned, practiced, and later applied to situations where tension or anger are experienced; that relaxation and arousal are incompatible responses and the client can learn to feel relaxed instead of aroused in difficult situations; and that developing this skill will require intensive, diligent practice.
2. A detailed deep muscle relaxation training exercise is then conducted. With the client seated in a comfortable recliner chair, usually in a dimly lit room removed from auditory distractions, the therapist guides him or her in a systematic relaxation exercise. The most frequently used procedure requires the client successively to tense and then relax various muscle groups, discriminating sensation differences between muscular tension and relaxation, and attempting to increase progressively feelings of relaxation. (A therapist guide or script for conducting such a relaxation-training exercise is found in Appendix III of this book.) A muscle relaxation practice session which follows this format requires approximately 25 minutes.
3. At the conclusion of the muscle relaxation exercise, and with the client continuing to relax, the therapist describes a relax-

ing imaginal scene. For example, the client might be told to imagine that s/he is lying on the soft, grassy ground of a meadow on a pleasant spring day, listening to the sound of a breeze in the trees, and feeling completely calm and tranquil. As the therapist describes the relaxing scene, the client is told to imagine that s/he is actually in it. Following this description, the parent continues to relax, and maintain the image. After several additional minutes, the practice session is concluded.

4. Throughout the practice exercise, the therapist both presents the relaxation instructions and simultaneously observes whether the client is performing muscular tension/relaxation movements correctly. Immediately following the conclusion of practice session, it is useful to discuss whether the client feels more relaxed, if any parts of his/her body were more difficult than others to relax, and whether the imaginal scene could be visualized. While clients often report feeling relaxed in even the first practice session, the therapist should emphasize that with practice, even greater relaxation is usually achieved.
5. Clients also practice the basic relaxation exercise on a daily basis at home between sessions. If the therapist makes an audiotape recording of the complete relaxation instruction (most easily accomplished by simply recording the procedure as it is conducted during the first training session), the client can play the tape and follow the same procedure at home. Most clients are advised to practice the full relaxation procedure once each day, and to pick a calm practice time when they will not be interrupted. During clinic sessions, the therapist reviews results of the client's daily practices and reinforces his/her continued skill practice.

When proficiency in self-relaxation with the tape-recorded directions is evident (based on client reports and by observation of the client's behavior during relaxation exercises), two modifications in the relaxation procedure are needed. The first is fading and discontinuing the use of verbal directions, both by the therapist and on the tape, as the client practices self-relaxation. Goldfried and Davison (1976) suggest that clients practice the full relaxation procedure (including all muscle tensing and relaxing, as well as imagery) without verbal guidance; after several weeks of daily direction-guided practice, most individuals will be able to complete the procedure by memory. Care should be taken to ensure that clients do not "rush" the pace of the practice session, and at least one self-directed exercise should be observed by the therapist. At-home practice without the recording continues on a daily basis, although periodic "booster" sessions using verbal directions can be used.

A second refinement, when the client is able to self-relax without directions, is reducing the period it takes to achieve relaxation. There are several ways this can be accomplished. One is for the individual to focus attention on each body part and simply relax it, without following the tense–relax sequence. Another, which can be combined with this "letting go" (Goldfried & Davison, 1976) process, is having the client focus on one salient, effective aspect of the relaxation procedure (such as deep, slow breathing or the calming imaginal scene) and then extend relaxation to the total body. Some experimentation may be needed for the client to discover his or her best "quick relaxation" procedure, and the therapist should explore what procedure works best for the parent. The aim, however, is to develop now and practice a technique that can induce relaxation in a much shorter period of time than was possible with the original procedure. When a client has mastered the skill of brief self-relaxation, it can be applied within situations that elicit anger and arousal.

7.2.1.2. In-Clinic Desensitization to Anger-Eliciting Cues

In his extensive line of treatment research on anger control, Novaco (1975, 1976, 1977, 1978) has described a systematic desensitizationlike procedure for "inoculating" clients against discrete cues that evoke anger. In a clinic session, the therapist first induces relaxation; because relaxation is a required component of this treatment, thorough relaxation training precedes desensitization. When the client has fully relaxed and is visualizing a calming imaginal scene, the therapist directs the client to imagine being in a situation that has, in the past, elicited a mild degree of annoyance or irritation. As the therapist describes the mildly annoying situation and imaginally "places" the client in it, the client continues to relax; if any arousal, anger, or anxiety is experienced during the scene presentation, the client signals the therapist (usually with an index finger movement) and is given directions to visualize himself or herself composed, relaxed, and coping calmly in that situation. This coping visualization is maintained for about 15 seconds, after which time the client stops visualizing the scene and returns to a state of relaxation, guided by therapist instructions to re-relax. The procedure is repeated with the same scene until the client experiences little anger arousal and can clearly visualize calm, coping behavior in the situation.

Earlier in this chapter, we described the construction of a hierarchy of anger-inducing situations. These situations can be used to create the scenes that are presented to the client in desensitization sessions, with the least anger-arousing scenes covered first and more potent elicitors of anger covered only in later sessions when the client has successfully mastered the earlier scenes. Treatment takes place over a number of clinic visits, with the pace determined by the client's success in becoming desensitized to imagined scenes of anger-arousing stimuli and visualizing himself/herself coping calmly with the presented situations. Readers familiar with traditional systematic desensitization will recognize the similarities between Novaco's procedure and that technique, including relaxation when descriptions of aversive stimuli are presented. Visualizing oneself coping in a calm, deliberate, and composed fashion in the troublesome situation adds a covert rehearsal element to the procedure and enables the client to practice, in imagination, how s/he will calmly handle the difficult situation.

Therapists who plan in-clinic desensitization for abusive parents should keep several considerations in mind. While Novaco has described the effectiveness of anger-control treatment that includes this component (Novaco, 1975, 1976, 1977, 1978), controlled studies have not yet applied it to the specific anger problems experienced by child-abusive parents. However, several investigators have noted the probable utility of techniques that desensitize abusive parents to stimuli which elicit anger (Doctor & Singer, 1978; Dubanoswki *et al.*, 1978;

Resick & Sweet, 1979), and data on abusive parents' heightened physiological arousal to aversive cues of child misbehavior (Disbrow *et al.*, 1977; Frodi & Lamb, 1980; Wolfe *et al.*, in press) suggest that this form of intervention will be useful for certain clients. Nonetheless, it must be viewed as a promising, but not yet empirically substantiated component of treatment for abusive parents.

A second issue, and one that applies to most forms of coping-skills treatment, is that clients also require training to help them develop the behavioral competencies needed to better handle situations that evoke anger. For example, while a parent might be taught to simply relax when a child screams and tantrums, relaxation is not likely to be a sufficient form of treatment unless the parent also learns how to handle the child's tantrums better. Thus, desensitization- or relaxation-based treatment should be combined with training to improve the client's behavioral skills for handling the situations which cause anger, whether these involve child-management skills or some other form of competency.

Finally, relaxation training and imaginal desensitization to aversive stimuli will be clinically effective only when the new skills are actually used in the natural environment. Therefore, we will next consider teaching parents to apply relaxation skills in the home setting.

7.2.1.3. Assignments to Apply Self-Relaxation Skills

To this point, the parent undergoing relaxation training to control anger has learned the basic skills of self-relaxation, including brief relaxation procedures, and may have undergone in-clinic desensitization to certain stimuli that elicit arousal. As these skills are acquired, the therapist can guide the client in the beginning to use them in difficult real-life situations.

Assignments to apply self-relaxation are most likely to be successful when they are focused on specific situations, when the client brings to sessions detailed information on how problems are handled, and when the therapist reinforces evidence of improved anger control by the parent. Just as situations included on the client's hierarchy can be used to determine scenes for in-clinic desensitization, the same situations can also be used to guide assignments to practice relaxation and coping skills at home. To illustrate, let us assume that a low-rated situation on a mother's anger hierarchy is the sound of her child's extended crying; this stimulus, according to the parent, evokes a mild degree of anger and irritation. An initial assignment for this parent might be to practice brief self-relaxation as soon as she notices any feelings of anger or annoyance when her child is crying. While the parent is becoming relaxed and calm in the situation she can also visualize *seeing herself* feeling comfortable and composed. Finally, when any anger has been reduced, the parent should decide what previously trained child-management technique is appropriate to use in the situation and implement it.

Whenever possible, assignments to practice self-relaxation should follow the graded anger hierarchy, with the parent first practicing the skill in situations which have led to only moderate anger in the past. In this manner, the client can have successful experiences coping with mild to moderate anger-evoking stimuli before s/he encounters more difficult self-control episodes. Naturally, however, relaxation skills should be used if an unexpected anger crisis situation develops unexpectedly and before it has been assigned.

Assignments to practice relaxation should always be accompanied by some form of anger-monitoring diary in which the parent records (1) any occasions when the targeted practice situation occurred, (2) what the parent did in each situation (i.e., followed the self-relaxation procedure), (3) how effectively anger feelings were controlled, and (4) whether other anger-producing situations took place between therapist visits. When recordings of this kind are maintained, the therapist and parent can together review details of all relevant anger situations and the manner in which they were handled. Successful reports of anger coping should be reinforced and encouraged, while the details of unsuccessful relaxation attempts will yield information on areas where additional training is needed. Finally, asking parents to record new situations that evoked anger provides data for additional scenes to be added to the anger hierarchy and to be targeted for future practice assignments.

7.2.2. Cognitive Training in Anger Control

Relaxation-based components of anger-control treatment can be seen as serving several functions, including induction of physiological calming, interruption of an immediate "aversive stimulus–violent response" behavior pattern, and desensitization of a client to cues that were previously associated with heightened arousal. As Novaco (1975) has stressed, anger responses are also mediated by cognitive components that can themselves be targeted for treatment.

Cognitive aspects of anger-control training are based on the broader work of Meichenbaum (Meichenbaum, 1974, 1975, 1977; Meichenbaum & Cameron, 1973), Mahoney (Mahoney, 1974, 1977; Mahoney & Arnkoff, 1977), Ellis (1973, 1977), and other cognitive-behavioral theorists. As we summarized in Chapter 3, these formulations emphasize that external events of any kind rarely affect complex human behavior directly; instead, cognitive-mediation processes (such as how one labels a situation, the self-statements and "private speech" one makes regarding the situation, and cognitive expectancies) also influence the behavior that will occur. Further, self-statements and self-instructions guide and shape the conduct of the individual.

With respect to anger, the cognitive processes that instigate, maintain, or heighten arousal might include any or all of the following: the labeling of one's feelings as anger ("I'm really mad at him now"), malevolent attributions concerning the other party's intent ("He's doing that just to anger me"), self-statements suggesting that one is unable to handle a situation effectively ("I don't know what to do . . . I'm losing control"), aggressive self-instructions ("I have to spank him now to teach him a lesson"), and maladaptive ruminations about unpleasant events ("I'm all alone now, thanks to him"). To the extent that such cognitions precede or accompany a child-abusive parent's violent behavior, they should also be targeted for intervention during anger-control training.

The assessment of cognitive behavior is difficult for several reasons. Unlike overt, observable actions, cognitions cannot be directly observed, and instead, must be inferred based on the client's verbal descriptions of what s/he is thinking. In addition, individuals appear to vary considerably in their ability to notice and describe what they are thinking; this is probably because certain cognitive processes (such as self-instructions) occur in a highly automatic, covert, and unlabeled or unverbalized manner. Novaco (1978) suggests that therapists recount some past situation where the client felt angry, ask the client to close his or her eyes, and "run a movie" of the anger experience with the client instructed to state all that s/he was thinking and feeling in that situation. The situations included in the client's anger hierarchy can each be examined in this way. Additionally, and following a discussion about the role of thoughts in anger responses, parents can be instructed not only to monitor situations where they experience anger between therapist visits, but also to observe carefully and record immediately their thoughts in those situations (Meichenbaum, 1977).

7.2.2.1. *Initial Training in Cognitive Modification*

The aims of cognitive modification in anger-control treatment are to teach clients to identify thoughts that increase their anger, cease engaging in those thoughts, and replace anger-arousing cognitions with self-statements facilitating calmness, control, and an appropriate handling of the difficult situation. As with other forms of skill training, this is accomplished through instruction, modeling, rehearsal, feedback/reinforcement, and application to real-life problems. As we will see, cognitive intervention is usually combined systematically with training in other aspects of anger control, such as relaxation.

When a parent understands the relationship of anger-related thoughts to actual episodes of anger or violence, and when there has been detailed discussion of the particular thoughts, self-statements, and cognitions exhibited by the client in past anger situations, training itself can begin. Since treatment requires that an individual learn to replace anger cognitions with more adaptive self-statements, developing a new repertoire of calming self-instructions for use in difficult situations is necessary. The therapist and client can together construct a written list of statements that might be used to cope with anger; the self-statements on this list should include instructions to remain calm and composed, to maintain emotional control in the situation, and to strengthen the likelihood of an appropriate handling of the problem that is eliciting anger. Some examples of coping self-statements include:

"Just stay calm."

"This is a little irritating to me, but I'm not really angry."

"I can handle this problem and will remain calm and collected as I decide how."

"She's just a child and while she is misbehaving, I know that it is not directed at me."

"Just breathe slowly, stay calm, and relax for a minute."

These types of self-statements can facilitate the maintenance of emotional control and reduction of anger. It is always important, however, to personalize coping statements to a parent's own anger-control problems and to request the client's assistance in developing self-instructions that will be most effective for him or her.

When a list of coping statements has been written, training can be initiated to help the parent rehearse them. Clinical research on anger control and cognitive-modification training (Meichenbaum, 1975, 1977; Novaco, 1975, 1978) indicates that it is important to have clients follow a series of steps in their rehearsal of new cognitions. First, the client is asked to imagine that s/he is in a situation; one scene from the less intense portion of the client's anger hierarchy can be selected for initial training. Next, the therapist encourages the client to notice and describe any anger thoughts or feelings that would ordinarily occur in that situation. As s/he identifies those anger cues, s/he should say the word "no" or "stop" to terminate them, and begin to say, aloud and slowly, several of the calm self-statements from the previously constructed list. At this point in training, the parent should rehearse self-statements by speaking them out loud (*overtly*). While the parent can initially read self-statements from a written practice list, each statement is spoken slowly, deliberately, and in such a way as to "convince" the client that it is true. Thus, the client is overtly instructing or telling himself to remain calm, at ease, and in emotional control. If the parent encounters difficulty in this overt practice phase, therapist modeling may be used to demonstrate the desired behavior.

The same scene can be rehearsed a number of times and several different anger scenes might be covered within the same session. It is extremely important for clients to understand that the purpose of overt rehearsal is to have them gain experience in calming themselves; for that reason, concentrating on the task and using the self-statements to alter the way they feel should always be stressed. After several practice attempts, the written list of statements is discontinued and clients can be encouraged to verbalize personal variations of the basic statements, rather than repeatedly "parrot" the same phrases.

When the client's overt performance of self-statements appears smooth, effective, and convincing, the training session can focus attention on *covert* rehearsal of the scenes. The aim in this transition is for clients to practice generating their self-statements in thought rather than aloud. Meichenbaum (1977) suggests that following successful overt rehearsal (with statements said aloud) clients perform the same scene with self-statements whispered softly rather than spoken in normal voice amplitude. Finally, situation rehearsal can be made entirely covert by having the individual think, rather than whisper, each statement or instruction. As rehearsal progresses from overt verbalizations to the practice of covert thoughts, clients should be encouraged to maintain the same pacing, detail, and concentration that characterized their earlier practice aloud.

Detailed guides for the use of cognitive-modification techniques have been published; therapists may wish to consult Meichenbaum (1977) or Novaco (1975) for further discussion of these treatment procedures. However, it is important for the therapist to bear in mind that comprehensive anger-control training relies on instruction in a combination of self-control elements, including cognitive modification, imaginal and physical relaxation, and desensitization to anger-arousing cues. Novaco (1975, 1976, 1978) suggests that practice cover all of these elements. For example, when clients have acquired basic relaxation skills, and when they are able to practice relaxation while visualizing themselves calmly handling a difficult situation, they can also rehearse the covert self-statements they will use in that situation. In this way, the parent practices in the training setting all of the anger-control techniques s/he will later apply in the natural environment.

At-home assignments to practice cognitive-modification skills can be easily combined with parents' home assignments to use relaxation. As the therapist and parent select situations from the anger hierarchy that have already been practiced in training, the parent can be directed to apply both relaxation and cognitive-modification skills in those situations at home. Throughout this application phase, the therapist should carefully review the parent's written self-monitoring records, seek specific information on how relaxation and cognitive-modification techniques were applied, and reinforce evidence of more adequate coping with anger. If the client encountered difficulty applying the skills in anger-provoking situations, discussion and additional practice may be required. In addition, new situations can be added to the anger hierarchy, and can be targeted for training and at-home practice whenever this becomes necessary.

7.2.3. Anger-Control Research with Abusive Families

Although abusive parents frequently injure their children during periods when they are angry and have lost emotional "control," and in spite of several recommendations that the anger-control problems of the parents be studied and directly treated (Doctor & Singer, 1978; Dubanowski *et al.*, 1978; Resick & Sweet, 1979), systematic evaluation of this component of child abuse treatment is still in its early stages. Several controlled interventions have included training in anger management as part of a larger treatment package. For example, Denicola and Sandler (1980) reported that the parents in two abusive families were taught to use deep muscle relaxation and cognitive-modification techniques during difficult interactions with their children; the same parents also received training in child-management skills. The combined anger-control–child-management intervention successfully improved the parents' rated skill during interactions with their children as well as the children's own behavior, although the relative contributions of anger-control and child-management training to this success could not be determined. Wolfe *et al.* (1981c) taught similar anger-control procedures when working with abusive parents in training groups. Once again, anger control was used in conjunction with child-management training, and the combined intervention resulted in improved parenting skills, reduced reports of child behavior problems, and no further instances of suspected abuse among treatment group subjects. Thus, when used with other skills-training techniques, anger-management strategies prove clinically useful for many abusive parents.

8

Intervening to Reduce Life-Style Risk Factors of Abusive Parents

To this point, we have considered the role of child-management and anger-control skill deficits as contributors to child abuse, and have discussed interventions for each. Since episodes of violence can often be directly traced to the parent's inability to handle his or her child's behavior nonviolently, specific treatment in these areas is logical and necessary for most abusive parents.

On the other hand, and as we saw in Chapters 2 and 3, there is evidence to suggest that many child-abusive families experience difficulties that extend beyond the immediate problems of knowing how to control their children and coping with anger. Life-style stressors such as excessive child care responsibilities, financial and economic disadvantage, parent social isolation, poor problem-solving skills, marital discord, and substance abuse have all been implicated as contributors to child abuse, especially by large-scale demographic studies (Gaines *et al.*, 1978; Garbarino, 1976; Garbarino & Sherman, 1980; Gelles, 1973; Gil, 1970, 1975; Smith *et al.*, 1974). To the extent that parents are significantly frustrated, angered, or preoccupied by difficulties in basic areas of everyday living, we might surmise that their resourcefulness and effectiveness in dealing with their children will also be impaired. While studies have not demonstrated that life-style stressors are either necessary or sufficient to produce child abuse, they may well create a background "triggering" context (Gil, 1975) that reduces the general coping skills of parents and exacerbates the likelihood of violence.

In this chapter, we will consider interventions to target certain life-style factors that have been empirically related to increased risk for child maltreatment. However, therapists working with abusive families should bear several issues in mind concerning these risk factors. First, since controlled research on how life-style stressors contribute to child abuse is still quite preliminary, therapists must rely on their own close assessment of a family's functioning to determine whether such factors are contributing to violence. Second, although the stressors considered here have been documented to occur more frequently among abusive than nonabusive families, this does not imply that a given abusive family is affected by all (or even any) of them. Some families may require a great deal of attention in these areas, while others may not. Finally, the reduction of life-style risk factors should be viewed as one component of a total intervention "package" that also includes attention to any immediate precipitants of abuse, such as child-management or anger-control problems.

8.1. EXCESSIVE CHILD-CARE DEMANDS

Abusive parents are frequently described as feeling overwhelmed and trapped by child-care demands (Giovannoni, 1971; Pelton, 1978), and several investigators have pointed out that these parents often have fewer available care alternatives than many nonabusive parents (Gelles, 1973; Gil, 1970). Presumably, the stress of excessive child-care responsibilities is greatest for parents who have large numbers of children, parents who are poor and unable to afford daycare or sitter services, and single-parent families where there is no spouse with whom to share or alternate duties. In these cases, the demands of daily child care may well be a source of stress and frustration to the overwhelmed parent. Interestingly, the social isolation frequently ascribed to abusive parents (Green, 1976; Helfer, 1973; Holmes *et al.*, 1975; Spinetta, 1978) may interact with insufficient child-care options to produce even greater stress: a parent who must stay at home with children will have less time to develop social relationship outside the home and may thereby develop fewer close friends and family members to assist in mutual, cooperative child-care assistance. It is difficult to leave a child with a trusted friend for an evening if one has few friends.

If a parent reports feeling overwhelmed by the daily responsibilities of child care, practical planning for assistance in this area is needed. Enrollment of the infant or preschool-age child in a daycare program is an effective way to reduce this source of stress. For families with limited financial resources, government-funded daycare programs such as Headstart, or cooperative child-care programs within the family's neighborhood should be explored. Even if arrangements for daily child care prove to be unfeasible, a plan that gives the parent even one or two mornings each week away from routine responsibilities may help to alleviate this stress.

Especially when working with single parents, child-care arrangements to permit occasional evenings out can also be investigated. Social activities of interest and importance to the parent (such as dating or spending time with friends) do not always take place during the daytime hours when most low-cost preschool programs operate. In our clinic, we find that young single parents, in particular, often feel frustrated and resentful when they cannot participate in activities during evening hours owing to continual child-care demands. In these cases, a therapist can work with the parent to explore options that allow occasional evenings away from the home. For families with sufficient financial resources, sitter or evening child-care programs should be considered; for those with limited resources, reciprocal child-care agreements with neighbors, friends, or relatives can be explored.

There has been a recognition in this society that parents often need and deserve "breaks" from their child-care responsibilities, and that being a good parent does not require divorcing oneself from activities outside the home. Abusive parents who feel trapped or overwhelmed by the demands of unabated child care may have even greater needs for regular periods away from their children; planning that encourages time away from the children can reduce this source of frustration.

8.2. SOCIAL ISOLATION

Child-abusive parents are often described as interpersonally isolated and lacking in adequate social supports (Green, 1976; Helfer, 1973; Holmes *et al.*, 1975; Parke & Collmer, 1975; Smith *et al.*, 1974; Spinetta, 1978; Young, 1964). Wahler's (1980) finding that parents trained in child-management skills had the fewest problems with their children on days when they had positive interactions with friends, and the greatest number of child problems on days when they were socially "insular," indicates that the presence of social supports may influence the number of aversive parent–child interactions in the home. Wahler (1980) has also suggested that since the parent social support variable appears to influence success in carrying out effective child-management techniques, individuals with an extremely limited range of social contacts may benefit from therapeutic attention to improve their own interpersonal relationships. A number of investigators have pointed out that treatment to improve relationships and reduce social isolation should be specifically considered in interventions with abusive parents (Fox, 1977; Friedman *et al.*, 1981; Kempe, 1973; Watkins & Bradbard, 1982).

While social support and positive friendships with others are widely recognized as contributors to personal adjustment, interventions to help socially isolated individuals develop relationships are still relatively uncommon in the psychological treatment literature. However, several treatment strategies may be useful with the socially isolated abusive parent. These include *home visitation arrangements, assignments to involve the parent in positive relationships outside the home, and social-skills training.*

8.2.1. Home Visitation

Kempe and his associates (Kempe, 1973; Kempe & Helfer, 1972) have described a program in which trained laypersons—including senior citizens and other volunteers—are "assigned" to visit a child-abusive family's home on a regular, frequent basis over an extended period of time. Spending between 4 and 10 hours each week with the family, the caregiver's role is to befriend the parent, to provide emotional support, to go shopping with the parent, to assist the parent in becoming more involved in social activities outside the home, and to model appropriate child-management techniques. In contrast to the formal home visits that might be made by a therapist or other professional, the assignment of a lay volunteer to an abusive parent is intended to provide a source of nonprofessional but positive social support (Fox, 1977; Kempe, 1973). One national child abuse program, termed Suspected Child Abuse and Neglect (SCAN), relies heavily on the use of screened but nonprofessional volunteers who spend time casually interacting with parents in abusive families. Preliminary evaluations of the SCAN program indicate that it does reduce the incidence of child maltreatment in these families and that parents respond favorably to the "befriending" provided by nonprofessional volunteers (Holmes & Kagel, 1977).

Home visitation programs of this type appear useful in the sense of ensuring that an isolated parent develops a relationship with at least one nonprofessional interested in his or her affairs. Because the volunteer "visitor" initiates and maintains contact with the parent, the task of developing social supports does not fall on the parent alone. Especially if they are well trained, nonprofessional volunteers can be a source of emotional support, can provide practical child-care and homemaking information to the parent (as well as information to the therapist on the family's at-home problems and skills), and can ease the parent's entry into other community social activities.

Whether these benefits will be realized depends on such factors as the volunteer's own interpersonal skills and his/her capacity to provide nonthreatening information to the parent. It also appears important that the abusive parent be able to relate to the volunteer as a friend, rather than simply a social worker surrogate; since home visitation programs typically assign volunteers *to* families, the manner in which a volunteer cultivates this relationship seems critical. Finally, establishing a relationship with an assigned volunteer does not address the long-term problem of deficient social supports for the isolated parent; only when the parent develops relationships with friends that s/he selects will the natural support network be strengthened. However, home visitation activities can be structured to facilitate this process.

8.2.2. Assignments to Increase Positive Social Activities outside the Home

For socially isolated parents, direct attention is needed to enhance the frequency and quality of relationships outside the home. Friedman *et al.* (1981) suggest asking isolated parents to record, in diary fashion, their positive social contacts so the therapist and client can discuss the adequacy of the client's supports. If positive social supports and relationships are a problem area for the parent, specific treatment can be planned. This might include an initial discussion of ways for the parent to develop friends (e.g., identifying and attending community or neighborhood social groups, joining the YWCA or YMCA, going to PTA functions, taking a credit or noncredit course in some area of interest to meet others with similar interests). As potential social outlets are identified, the therapist can make assignments for the client to investigate and pursue them. There are no "hard" guidelines for specific ways for helping a parent broaden his or her repertoire of social supports, since planning in this area must take into account the individual's preferences, interests, skills, and resources. However, the consistent aim of intervention is to increase the number of gratifying, positive social contacts with others and to decrease client feelings of isolation, loneliness, and frustration.

Special attention and planning are needed for parents who have unusual isolation problems. For example, isolated single parents may require treatment attention to help them establish dating relationships or may benefit from involvement in church or community support programs for single parents. Those who are recently divorced may find it useful to participate in support groups for the "newly single." Therapists treating parents with such specialized support needs should, of course, become familiar with community programs that can address their clients' difficulties.

8.2.3. Social-Skills Training

Many parents who are socially isolated will benefit from fairly direct discussion, problem-solving, practical planning, and assignments to broaden their interpersonal support resources. However, some individuals who lack social supports also lack the skills needed to develop relationships with others effectively. The parent who is anxious or unskilled when meeting others, the parent who comes across to other people as hostile and unfriendly, or the individual who is extremely shy may be unable to follow through on even well-planned assignments to meet other people owing to social-skills deficits. In these cases, basic training to enhance the client's interpersonal skills repertoire is needed before successful relationships can be formed.

Resick and Sweet (1979) point out that while social-skills training has not been used extensively with abusive individuals, those parents who have difficulty establishing supportive social contacts may well benefit from treatment of this kind. In particular, training to improve conversational skills (Minkin, Braukman, Minkin, Timbers, Timbers, Fixsen, Phillips, & Wolf, 1976; Kelly, 1982a), date-initiation skills (Arkowitz, 1977; Curran, 1977; Heimberg, Madsen, Montgomery, & McNabb, 1980), or assertiveness (Hersen, Eisler, & Miller, 1973; Galassi, Galassi, & Litz, 1974; Kelly, 1982a; Linehan, Goldfried, & Goldfried, 1979) can be useful for some parents who encounter difficulties forming everyday relationships with others. In a recent study reported by Scott *et al.* (1982), social-skills training was one intervention element for an abusive parent whose episodes of violence were closely associated with frustrating relationships with other adults in her life.

All child-abusive parents are not socially isolated. However, since abusive individuals are more likely to have inadequate social-support resources than other parents (Giovannoni & Billingsley, 1970; Young, 1964), and because social insularity predicts problems with children in the home (Wahler, 1980), systematic efforts to improve the interpersonal relationships of isolated abusive parents seem warranted.

8.3. ECONOMIC STRESS

Economic stress is a widely cited characteristic of families who mistreat children (Garbarino, 1976; Garbarino & Sherman, 1980), and several investigators have suggested that by alleviating the level of socioeconomic stress on families, the frequency of child maltreatment will also be reduced (Gelles, 1973; Gil, 1975). The exact manner in which economic disadvantage contributes to child abuse has not received close attention, although economic difficulties would appear to function as a direct stressor on the family (e.g., causing increased anger due to worries about finances) and, at the same time, may contribute to other everyday living problems (by, for example, reducing the family's access to paid child-care alternatives, limiting the parent's opportunity to engage in social or work activities outside the home, or creating overcrowded and substandard housing conditions). Consequently, intervention with low-income families often requires efforts to reduce the level of economic stress that they experience.

Dubanowski *et al.* (1978) suggest that therapists pursue the goals of reducing immediate, short-term financial pressures on the family and then developing longer-range plans that can more permanently alleviate the parent's economic difficulties. Both of these goals require the therapist to be familiar with social service and employment resources in the community, or to collaborate with other professionals who do have such knowledge.

8.3.1. Short-Term Intervention Strategies

For families with severe economic difficulties, the therapist should first determine whether the parents are receiving all of the financial and social welfare program benefits to which they are entitled. Examples of these services include general assistance (welfare) payments, Aid for Families with Dependent Children (AFDC), food stamps, Medicaid, and unemployment compensation. Less well-known sources of short-term aid available to some low-income families include reduced-rent or subsidized housing, financial assistance to meet utility bills, government-sponsored daycare, and a range of crisis services for families in extreme distress. Clients can be directed to the appropriate welfare agency to determine their eligiblity for these services, or the therapist can work directly with the parent in locating possible sources of immediate assistance.

Other nonwelfare avenues for reducing immediate financial stress can also be explored. Divorced or separated parents who are not receiving child-support payments may require legal assistance to obtain this source of income, while those who have lost spouses owing to death may be entitled to social security or veteran's survivor benefits. Parents burdened by extreme financial indebtedness can consult with a community legal aid office to discuss ways to restructure debt payments or initiate bankruptcy proceedings. The possibility of short-term loans from family members, friends, or lending agencies might also be considered.

While these steps can provide financial crisis relief, they will not solve the longer-term economic problems faced by most low-income families. Therefore, the therapist should also assist the parent in developing more enduring solutions for reducing economic stress.

8.3.2. Longer-Term Intervention Strategies

Unemployment, underemployment, and living expenses which exceed income are the most probable causes of family financial stress. For this reason, the therapist treating an economically stressed abusive family may be called upon to help the parents gain the skills needed for successful job finding and job maintenance.

If a parent has an extremely limited history of past employment, has skills suitable only for a vocation for which there is little demand, or has insufficient experience and education to compete in the open job market, participation in a vocational training or remedial educational program may be needed before the individual can find employment. A variety of different vocational training, vocational retraining, work experience, and educational programs are offered through state employment services, public welfare departments, and adult educational facilities. Certain programs provide not only work experience or training, but also pay the adult while s/he is in training and cover certain incidental expenses such as child care. Since few therapists are in a position to be aware of all such resources and the eligibility requirements for each, consultation with appropriate employment and welfare agency staff is often needed.

While some clients are unemployed because they lack basic vocational or educational competencies, deficient job-finding skills can be problematic for many individuals. In this case, the parent is unable to find work because s/he does not use effective skills for seeking employment, rather than because the client is fundamentally "unemployable." Therapists can often assist the parent in seeking work more effectively.

8.3.2.1. Training in Job-Finding Skills

The process of finding employment can be task analyzed into a number of different skills or competencies. Knowledge and use of appropriate job lead sources (e.g., contacting friends who may know of openings, using the Yellow Pages to locate potential categories of employers, following want ads, using employment service materials), having a well-constructed résumé, speaking effectively on the telephone to potential employers, completing application forms correctly, and interviewing skillfully are all requisite competencies of successful job-seeking (Azrin, Flores, & Kaplan, 1975; Jones & Azrin, 1973). Problems in any of these areas can reduce the client's likelihood of obtaining a job.

Parents with an unsuccessful history of finding employment should be carefully evaluated to ensure that they can exhibit effective job-seeking skill behavior. Asking clients to complete sample application forms, to show the therapist a copy of their résumé (or, if they do not have one, prepare a typed résumé), to demonstrate the effective use of resources to locate possible openings, and to role play telephone contact and job interview skills are all useful ways to assess job-seeking skill level (Azrin *et al.*, 1975; Hollandsworth, Glazeski, & Dressel, 1978; Jones & Azrin, 1973; Kelly, 1982b; Kelly, Wildman, & Berler, 1980). Problems identified in any of these areas can be targeted for specific training and practice.

Employment research indicates that the most promising job leads are usually obtained by making contacts and inquiries to friends or acquaintances who work. Employment often follows a period of high-rate, systematically planned job-seeking that includes making large numbers of daily contacts and following up closely on all possible leads (Azrin *et al.*, 1975; Kelly, 1982b). Additionally, well-developed and carefully practiced job interview skill appears to be a salient predictor of whether an individual will be hired for a position (Cohen & Etheridge, 1975; Drake, Kaplan, & Stone, 1975). For these reasons, the therapist treating an unemployed child-abusive parent may wish to devote time both to rehearsing important job-seeking skills and ensuring that the client actually seeks employment in a systematic, high-rate manner (Wodarski, 1981).

8.3.2.2. Intervention with Parents Who Are Working

Some individuals are able to find jobs but experience considerable difficulty keeping them. While the training of job-*seeking* skills has received primary attention in the research literature, employment retention (or job-*keeping*) is an important issue for some financially stressed persons. In several studies, between 17–25% of chronically unemployed single parents with children who found jobs lost them within 30 days (Kelly, 1982b; Meehan & Ganson, 1982), suggesting that the skills needed to obtain employment may be different than those needed to retain it.

If the financially stressed abusive parent has a history of frequent job loss, attention should be directed toward identifying the causes of this problem and providing appropriate intervention to reduce the likelihood of continued loss of employment. Possible areas for exploration include: inadequate child care and lack of reliable transportation to the job, resulting in high absenteeism; poor handling of interpersonal relationships or conflicts with co-workers, supervisors, or customers at work; and the selection of an inappropriate job (e.g., a job which provides few gratifications, is uninteresting to the client, is in a low-demand area and makes the client susceptible to layoff, or simply requires job skills that the client lacks). All of these are common reasons for job loss and can be appropriate target areas for treatment.

Finally, having employment does not preclude the possibility of experiencing financial stress. If a family's income is insufficient to meet its expenses, intervention to reduce the disparity is needed. Some investigators have suggested that financially stressed abusive families may benefit from assistance in budgeting and everyday economic planning (Dubanowski *et al.*, 1978). Additionally, possibilities for increasing the income of the family should be explored; these strategies might include seeking a raise, changing jobs, obtaining further training, and determining whether the parent qualifies for public assistance for the "working poor."

Unemployment, poverty, and economic disadvantage are obviously complex and substantial social problems. However, since economic stress predicts an increased likelihood of child maltreatment, abusive families with this risk factor may benefit from practical intervention to improve their socioeconomic functioning.

8.4. MARITAL DISCORD

In child-abusive families where the parental relationship is intact, an elevated frequency of marital conflict between the spouses has been noted (Bennie & Sclare, 1969; Green *et al.*, 1974; Ory & Earp, 1980; Smith, 1975; Young, 1964). Reports of actual physical violence between spouses are described as occurring more often among child-abusive families (Nurse, 1964; Green *et al.*, 1974), and one project found that periods of high couple conflict preceded incidents of child abuse (Bennie & Sclare, 1969). While studies of marital discord have often relied on clinical observation rather than controlled empirical study (Berger, 1980), at least some abusive families are characterized by both violence directed toward the child and violence exhibited between the spouses. For these families, treatment of marital difficulties may be useful in reducing the level of stress and frustration experienced by the couple, increasing emotional support within the marriage, and providing a social environment conducive to the use of appropriate child-management skills (Friedman *et al.*, 1981; Moore, 1975).

A number of writers have advocated marital therapy as one component of the child-abusive family's treatment (Doctor & Singer, 1978;

Kempe *et al.*, 1962). Unfortunately, no reports have yet provided empirical data on the outcome of this treatment component. For this reason, it is important for the therapist to rely on a functional assessment of the family to determine whether couple conflict is a context variable that increases the likelihood of child-directed violence. If child-abusive incidents occur during periods of couple discord and conflict, or if chronic difficulties between the spouses are likely to interfere with the implementation of other treatment elements, attention to the marital relationship is indicated.

8.5. PROBLEM-SOLVING SKILL DEFICITS

All of the life-style risk factors discussed in this chapter share an area of commonality: the parent's adaptive skill is reduced, and the possibility of violence is exacerbated, due to the presence of an external problem or life stressor of some kind. In some cases, the therapist can intervene directly as a service resource for the stressed client; assisting a parent in applying for a previously unknown welfare benefit or locating for a parent the name of a low-cost daycare program are examples of this direct service role. More frequently, therapists working with child-abusive families teach their clients specific skills for altering stressful life circumstances. Examples of this skills-training approach include helping the unemployed parent practice and apply job-seeking competencies, assisting the socially isolated parent acquire skills for broadening his or her interpersonal support network, or working with discordant couples to teach them how to resolve marital conflicts without violence. Through these intervention strategies, the stressed parent will hopefully develop the skills to alleviate life-style frustrations and be capable of better parenting and improved overall functioning.

Since some abusive parents appear to be overwhelmed by difficult conditions in their lives, we might posit a final kind of intervention for reducing life-style stress. Over the past ten years, a great deal of clinical research effort has been directed to training persons in *problem-solving skills.* The rationale for this treatment is that coping effectively with everyday frustrations or obstacles requires a series of cognitive and behavioral skills, and that individuals who are unable to solve the problems affecting them often lack the skills to do so (D'Zurilla & Goldfried, 1971; Platt, Spivak, Altman, & Altman, 1974). Most clinical applications of problem-solving training focus on teaching clients several steps for resolving difficulties: (1) identifying whether a situation is a problem, (2) generating or "brainstorming" a large variety of possible solutions to the problem, (3) weighing each alternative and anticipating the probable consequences of it, (4) selecting the best alternative or solution to the problem, and (5) following up on the course of action that was selected (see D'Zurilla & Goldfried, 1971, or Spivak, Platt, & Shure, 1976, for a detailed discussion of this process). Although the step-by-step nature of this problem-solving process appears quite straight forward, it actually requires a number of complex cognitive and behavioral competencies (such as gaining sufficient practical information so that one can generate possible solutions, being able to anticipate the consequences of various courses of action, and having the behavioral skills to carry out a planned solution). For this reason, teaching clients to use effective problem-solving skills ordinarily requires relatively intensive intervention.

Problem-solving training has been applied to a wide range of difficulties, including those experienced by children, adolescents, socially isolated individuals, delinquents, and psychiatric patients (D'Zurilla & Goldfried, 1971; Platt *et al.*, 1974; Spivak *et al.*, 1976). Interestingly, although child-abusive parents are frequently characterized as being overwhelmed by the stress of everyday problems in living, few interventions have included specific efforts to teach these parents more effective problem-solving skills. One exception is the project of Scott *et al.* (1982), where an abusive mother was given training in basic problem-solving, in addition to treatment of her child-management, anger, and social difficulties. The situations practiced in the problem-solving component of treatment involved life difficulties that the parent actually experienced, such as deciding what type of job to seek, whether to move, or how to handle problems with her landlord. Tape recorded ratings demonstrated that following training, the parent was able to generate more solutions to each practical problem situation and able to select solutions with a higher judged likelihood of succeeding that she had before treatment.

Training in the use of effective problem-solving skills may well be useful for those abusive parents who lack the ability to handle everyday difficulties they encounter successfully. As with other treatments to reduce life-style stressors, there remains a need to better evaluate the clients for whom this intervention will be useful and the extent to which it can reduce the likelihood of frustration and violence in the family.

9

Interdisciplinary Team Coordination in Abuse Cases

A number of different helping professionals are typically involved with the child-abusive family. As we saw in Chapter 1, the manner in which a parent is first identified as abusive and enters the social or child welfare "system" is usually multidisciplinary in nature: *physicians* or other medical staff often make the initial judgment that an injury is nonaccidental, *welfare caseworkers* investigate the family, *judicial personnel* evaluate child welfare needs and make decisions related to the child's safety, and *mental health professionals* (including psychologists, social workers, and family counselors) provide ongoing treatment to the family. Even after the family's identification and entry into the intervention system, other consultations take place among the various professionals involved with the case: courts periodically have hearings to review information about the family's intervention and overall progress in reducing conditions of risk to the child; caseworkers need information from the therapist regarding the family's progress in treatment; physicians may be called upon to evaluate the child's physical condition from time to time; and specialized social service resources for the family may need to be obtained (such as child care, public assistance, and employment assistance).

We can speculate that there are at least two reasons for the interdisciplinary nature of child abuse intervention. The first is that child abuse is itself defined in our society as a multidimensional problem that requires the involvement of legal, medical, psychological, and social welfare authorities. The second reason is that abusive families often have a variety of different intervention needs. These families can have multiple problems and, therefore, often require behavioral-psychological treatment, child-management training, social service intervention, child-protection planning, and similar services. Few professionals, even when well-trained, have sufficiently broad expertise and knowledge to function effectively as the sole intervention agent for a child-abusive family with multiple problems.

If a number of different professionals are involved in a family's treatment, there is a need for careful coordination among them. This is especially true when the problem is child abuse and involves what can be life-threatening situations for the youngster. Without effective interdisciplinary communication, mental health therapists may be unaware of significant aspects of a family's social history; caseworkers responsible for overall intervention planning may be unaware of the nature and duration of psychological or behavioral treatment the parents require; and court officials may have difficulty obtaining important information on the parents' compliance with a required intervention. However, all of these problems can be minimized if effective and clear communication channels are developed among the various professionals involved in a family's intervention.

Since this book is for therapists treating child-abusive families, we will focus on coordination issues that directly involve the therapist. Some of these issues will apply primarily when the therapist is with an agency other than the one which is actually responsible for child abuse investigation; examples include mental health center, family service center, or child clinic staff who are requested by a child welfare worker to provide treatment services. Other coordination matters apply to therapists, such as child-protective service social workers, who provide treatment and also have primary responsibility in overall planning for the family. Regardless of who the therapist is, there will undoubtedly be the need for communication with court judicial authorities, physicians and medical personnel, social welfare agencies, or community support programs. We will now consider how therapists can develop effective case information-sharing with each of these groups.*

9.1. RELATIONSHIPS WITH JUDICIAL AUTHORITIES

In the child-protective area, a primary responsibility of the court is to ensure the safety and well-being of the child. Decisions about child placement and custody are made to protect the minor, and courts often order a family to obtain various forms of assistance and treatment in order to maintain (or to regain) custody of the child. Thus, there is an explicit or implicit contingency relationship: the family will receive something (continued child custody, the return of a removed child, or the removal of the authorities from the family's affairs) when they demonstrate that the child's safety and well-being are no longer at risk. The child welfare agency responsible for handling cases of child maltreatment usually oversees the implementation of the intervention; in some cases, courts give the agency considerable latitude for developing the intervention program in which a family must participate. A court might, for example, order a family to participate in an unspecified program to be developed and managed by the child welfare agency caseworker.

If a therapist is treating a family as part of that family's court-ordered intervention, the therapist will be ordinarily called upon to provide periodic progress information to the authorities. This communication can be in the form of written reports or it can involve testimony at more formal, legal hearings about the family. Depending on the local child welfare system, therapists may make their reports directly to the court or, alternatively, to the welfare agency that implements the court's orders.

*Although persons, including professionals, can report in good faith cases of suspected child abuse without the threat of litigation for breaking confidentiality, routine disclosure of information about a family requires the completion of appropriate releases of information. It is advisable for a therapist to obtain written permission before discussing the parent's status or progress with the staff of other agencies.

9.1.1. Providing Treatment Information to Court Authorities

In order to reach conclusions about a child's safety, child welfare legal authorities usually require two types of information from a therapist. The first is data on the family's participation in the therapy intervention, and the second is information about the nature of treatment and progress toward alleviating the conditions that had caused the child to be at risk.

With regard to parent participation in treatment, it is important for the therapist to maintain accurate records of the number of sessions scheduled with the family, the number of appointments actually attended, and the number that were missed due to cancellations or no-shows. If home visits were included in the intervention, the frequency of these should also be reported. While documentation of the number of sessions that parents attend in relation to those they miss is not a comprehensive indicator of their participation in treatment, it does provide a quantified, objective measure of the family's cooperation and the amount of therapy attention they actually received.

Treatment progress reports made to courts or to the child welfare agency implementing a court's orders should also describe the apparent antecedents of the family's violence and the form of treatment being conducted or planned for each. As an example, if case assessment indicates deficits in the parent's child-management skills and anger-control skills, as well as context frustration owing to joblessness, the report should detail how each of these problem areas is being addressed.

Treatment progress reports are most useful when they provide descriptions in a quantified, objective, and behaviorally based manner. This can be accomplished by providing specific information on: (1) *the type of therapy program being used* to address each problem area that was an apparent antecedent of violence, such as child-management training, anger-control treatment, or assistance in developing job-finding skills; (2) *the manner by which treatment is being implemented* (e.g., through weekly home visits and clinic visits where the therapist discusses, models, and asks the parent to practice nonviolent ways to handle child misbehavior); (3) *objective evidence of behavior change* that indicates whether the likelihood of future violence is reduced and presents any available data confirming this change; and (4) *areas where further treatment is necessary,* including continued treatment that will be provided by the therapist or recommendations for other forms of family assistance that the therapist may not be able to provide directly (e.g., providing the parent with formal vocational-training assistance).

9.1.2. Requesting Changes in Court-Ordered Plans

In some cases, the therapist who has been treating child-abusive parents may find it desirable to request a change in some aspect of the court-ordered intervention plan for a family. For example, if a child was removed from the home owing to excessively harsh parental discipline, and if the parents have demonstrated gains in their knowledge of appropriate child management, it will be necessary for them to have contact with the child in order to be able to actually practice new parenting skills. If arrangements for supervised visitation were not made in an initial court order, or if a series of progressively longer visitation periods are desirable, the therapist may wish to make such recommendations.

It is also possible to link demonstrated progress in treatment to increasing amounts of parental contact with a child who had been removed from the home; this has the function of reinforcing parent behavior change, providing opportunities for the parent to practice coping or management skills with the child physically in the home, and gradually returning the family to its normal state with all members present. If such recommendations are made, they should be based on clear evidence that the child is no longer at risk; this evidence might include increased parent knowledge of appropriate child-management principles, successful performance of anger-control techniques, or reduced stress on the family, depending on which factors were responsible for past episodes of violence. Preliminary home visits by the child should always be closely supervised by the therapist or family caseworker, especially if the prior episodes of abuse were serious.

9.2. RELATIONSHIPS WITH MEDICAL PERSONNEL

As Steele (1976) has pointed out, the opinion of a pediatrician or other physician is needed to make the physical determination that an injury is nonaccidental in all but the most blatant cases of child abuse. Not only are most cases of abuse first documented by physicians and other medically trained professionals, but also physical reexamination of a previously abused child may be necessary to determine that continuing injuries are not being sustained. New occurrences of suspicious injury (such as bruises, cuts, fractures, or burns) to a youngster who had been maltreated in the past should always be investigated by a physician. Even when there is no reason to suspect continuing abuse, a follow-up physical evaluation of the previously abused child can provide collaborative information that the youngster is not sustaining additional, nonobvious injuries.

While therapists treating child-abusive families may require the periodic case consultation of pediatricians, it is also important for therapists to make local medical personnel aware of the types of treatment services they can provide to abusive families. In spite of the increased attention recently given to child abuse identification in the medical literature, and even though all states now have enacted mandatory abuse reporting laws, there are undoubtedly a large number of abuse cases that go unreported. One reason for nonreporting is that some physicians may be unsure whether referred families, especially those who have not blatantly injured their children, will receive useful, effective, and acceptable forms of intervention assistance. If therapists who treat abusive families establish closer ties to local medical personnel and better explain the types of intervention they conduct, it is likely that a larger proportion of these families will be referred for treatment.

9.3. RELATIONSHIPS WITH SOCIAL WELFARE AUTHORITIES

As we discussed earlier, some therapists treating child-abusive families are employed by government social welfare agencies, while others are outside the traditional social welfare agency system. Consequently, therapists have varying degrees of familiarity with the social service resources available in their community; those with little knowledge of such community resources will often find it useful to consult with social service staff who have direct knowledge of needed assistance programs. Public assistance caseworkers, welfare or employment/vocational service counselors, homemakers and health department visiting nurses, and similar types of workers can often provide practical, direct assistance in meeting the social service support needs of economically distressed abusive families.

In Chapter 8, we discussed the possible role of socioeconomic stress as a contributor to frustration and violence in certain abusive families. Since social welfare staff are often familiar with programs that can reduce life-style condition stressors, the therapist should evaluate whether supportive services in social problem areas are needed:

Is the family receiving all short-term public assistance benefits for which they are eligible? Consultation between the parent and a caseworker in the county public welfare department is necessary.

Does the parent lack basic homemaking and child-care skills? Assistance through the welfare department or public health department may be available.

Does the parent lack basic vocational skills? Participation in basic education and vocational training programs may be needed. The local welfare department or employment service usually determines eligibility for these programs; some vocational programs provide other assistance, such as child care or daily travel allowances, while the parent participates in them.

Does the parent have vocational skills but cannot find a job? In addition to counseling in job-seeking skills, the assistance of a government employment service agency may be useful. Eligibility for unemployment compensation can be determined by the same agency.

Is low-cost child-care assistance needed? If informal child care with friends, neighbors, or relatives cannot be arranged, welfare caseworkers can provide information on government-funded or nonprofit child-care resources, including Headstart.

To the extent that a child-abusive family experiences economic or social stress problems that are outside the therapist's primary area of competence, it is appropriate to seek consultation from other professionals who may be able to meet difficult social service needs. The development of contacts and relationships with these staff is important for ensuring a comprehensive intervention, especially with socioeconomically disadvantaged families whose environmental circumstances contribute to general life frustration.

Therapists sometimes treat families at the request of a social welfare agency that is legally responsible for overseeing the management of all reported child abuse cases. In these instances, the family may have both a primary welfare department caseworker (to meet their social service needs) and a therapist (to provide specialized counseling and mental health services). This arrangement requires unusually close and frequent collaboration between the caseworker and the therapist so that each can share information on the family's functioning, assess whether the family is exhibiting improved skills, determine significant problem areas that require continued attention, and plan how those areas will be addressed in treatment.

9.4. RELATIONSHIPS WITH COMMUNITY SUPPORT GROUPS

While welfare and other institutional agencies can meet some basic needs of the most economically stressed abusive families, an improved social support network in the community can benefit other parents. "Social supports" can be defined as the interpersonal resources to which an individual can turn in order to meet personal needs in everyday living. In contrast to welfare services provided by an agency or counseling provided by a therapist, social support groups are generally nonprofessional in nature, are based on individuals' voluntary participation in them, and are intended to bring the individual more positive contact with others. Since demographic studies have empirically related an increased incidence of child abuse to a paucity of community supports and resources (Gabarino, 1976;

Garbarino & Sherman, 1980), the abusive family lacking effective social supports may benefit from attention in this area. In order to direct clients to possible sources of social support, the therapist must first become aware of existing community resources and then "match" a given family to relevant resources.

There are *no a priori* guidelines for determining the social support needs of clients; instead, treatment efforts in this area must be preceded by a careful analysis of the individual's problems and an assessment of how a nonprofessional support group might assist the individual. While resources vary from community to community, the following types of organizations are useful for some clients:

Parents without Partners, or similar support organizations for single parents.

Singles groups, often conducted by churches, provide an opportunity for presently unmarried adults to meet and socialize with others.

Church activities, especially those of a social nature, which permit parents, couples, and children to interact with others.

Neighborhood community centers, oriented toward social activities, community civic endeavors, or neighborhood improvement projects.

The YMCA/YWCA, Boys' Clubs, and similar groups, which offer recreational and social programs for both children and adults.

Big Brothers and Big Sisters, programs that may be especially useful for providing an adult companion and role model to the child in a single-parent family.

Alcoholics Anonymous, a well-known community support program for adults with alcohol abuse problems.

Parents Anonymous, the peer support group comprised of child-abusive parents who discuss their own violent behavior and provide one another with support to overcome continued family violence.

Social support groups such as these exist in most communities and the therapist treating child-abusive families should seek out information about them. With the exception of Parents Anonymous, none of these programs is primarily oriented toward child-abusive families. However, because they are useful resources for clients with specialized needs (e.g., single parents, parents with few social outlets, families having little social–recreational contact with other families), therapists may wish to ask parents to involve themselves in appropriate social support groups.

10

Directions for Preventive Intervention

For clinicians working with child-abusive families, treatment of the client family is often the immediate, pressing, and understandable priority. However, since annual child abuse incidence estimates range from a conservative 60,000 cases (Education Commission of the States, 1973) upward to one-half million cases (Helfer & Kempe, 1976; Light, 1973), it is evident that prevention also merits much closer attention. Even with recent improvements in child abuse reporting, treatment, and follow-up, many maltreating families are never officially identified as abusive and will never receive treatment; even if it were somehow possible to identify all abusive families, the resources of child welfare agencies and mental health facilities would be hard pressed to treat all of them comprehensively. Just as primary prevention and early intervention are the goals of many mental health and social welfare programs (Geismar, 1969; Klein & Goldston, 1977; Rapoport, 1961), successful efforts to reduce the incidence of child-directed violence will prove to be more humane and, presumably, more effective than treating the relatively small proportion of cases that presently come to professionals' attention.

Approaches for prevention are always derived from a broader conceptualization about the causes of a particular problem. Thus, the population targeted in a prevention program and the nature of the intervention approach depend on what factors are seen as saliently contributing to the problem one seeks to prevent. In the case of child abuse, prevention strategies fall under three major categories: approaches that are based on psychopathology (psychiatric) models, approaches based on sociological models, and approaches that are based on a social-learning and interactional conceptualization of abuse.

As we saw in Chapter 3, the psychiatric model of child abuse attributes the occurrence of child-directed violence to disturbances in the abusive parent's personality makeup. Consequently, prevention programs based on this model include efforts to (1) detect those parents whose personality and psychological makeup dispose them to behave violently toward their children and (2) intervene with families to reduce the likelihood that children will develop psychological traits that might lead them to become abusive parents in the future. In these ways, prevention would focus largely on detecting and altering parent psychopathology risk variables.

Unfortunately, a number of factors complicate prevention programs based on this psychiatric model. While many different personality characteristics have been ascribed to child-abusive parents (see reviews by Berger, 1980; Shorkey, 1978; Spinetta & Rigler, 1972), efforts to predict empirically whether an individual is abusive or nonabusive based on personality variables have yielded largely negative or inconsistent findings (Floyd, 1975; Gaines *et al.*, 1978; Paulson *et al.*, 1974; Wright, 1976). In the absence of reliable, empirically based predictive criteria, it is very difficult to determine what personality "types" should be targeted by prevention programs. Further, although a small percentage of abusive parents do exhibit signs of severe psychopathology such as psychosis or sociopathy (Bell, 1973; Friedman *et al.*, 1981; Kempe & Kempe, 1978), it is not clear that these disturbed parents abuse their children more frequently than do other parents. As a result, a child abuse prevention program targeted simply to individuals who exhibit clear-cut emotional disorders may have little impact on overall rates of child maltreatment.

Prevention efforts based on sociological formulations of child abuse do have more empirical support, chiefly from larger-scale studies that demonstrate relationships between socioeconomic/community resource problems and child abuse incidence (Garbarino, 1976; Garbarino & Sherman, 1980; Gil, 1970). From a sociological perspective, the prevention of child abuse is linked to strategies for reducing the stress on families owing to poverty and unemployment, improving community services and social resources, providing more adequate child-care alternatives, and altering public attitudes that favor the use of punitive approaches in child rearing (Gil, 1971, 1975; Giovannoni, 1971). However, research to date has not yet established whether broad intervention to reduce conditions of poverty and social-community disadvantage per se will also reduce the incidence of child abuse (Resick & Sweet, 1979).

10.1. A SOCIAL LEARNING–INTERACTION MODEL OF PREVENTION

Earlier, it was argued that single-factor explanations of child abuse, including both psychiatric and sociological theories, are relatively narrow in focus and represent oversimplified models that account for relatively few cases of abuse. Alternatively, child-directed violence can be conceptualized as a behavior pattern with multiple antecedents that often involve the parent's child-management skill deficits, lack of knowledge about children, anger expression problems, and reduced adaptive functioning owing to the presence of life stressors (Belsky, 1978; Burgess, 1979; Dubanowski *et al.*, 1978; Parke & Collmer, 1975). As we have seen, this social-learning–interactional model gives rise to a number of specific case treatment interventions including child-management skills training, anger- and stress-management treatment, and therapeutic efforts to reduce life-style risk factors such as social isolation, joblessness, and poor problem-solving skills. The same conceptual formulation that underlies these case treatments also suggests various larger-scale preventive interventions that may prove effective in reducing the incidence of child maltreatment.

Before discussing prevention strategies, several more general issues should be noted. First, if child abuse is determined by multiple antecedents, it is unlikely that a prevention program focusing on only one causal factor will be effective for all families. As an example, programs to educate young adults on basic child development and child care may have an impact on cases of family violence that would occur because the parents had unrealistic expectations about their children's developmental competencies; the same program might have little impact on child maltreatment that occurs for reasons not addressed in this kind of single-factor prevention program. Presumably, prevention efforts will be most successful when they are comprehensive and cover a range of risk factors, or when they address those risk factors that are most salient contributors to abuse.

A second and related issue is an absence of empirical data on the effectiveness of child abuse prevention programs. While a number of writers have argued for specific programs to prevent abuse (Alvy, 1975; Galdston, 1965; Gil, 1975; Sundel & Homan, 1979), very few controlled outcome data are presently available from which to evaluate what kind of programs will have the maximum prevention impact. In fact, the effectiveness of *any* primary child abuse prevention program has yet to be established on a large applied scale. Just as there is a need for continuing empirical research on the clinical *treatment* of child-abusive families, efforts to evaluate the impact of primary *prevention* strategies in this area are also badly needed.

Until controlled program evaluation data are obtained, any discussion of child abuse prevention must be regarded as preliminary and tentative. However, based on a social-learning–interactional model, it is possible to identify at least three major areas where prevention efforts can be logically focused and evaluated. These areas involve the preventive modification of *parent risk factors, child risk factors,* and *situational and stress risk factors.*

10.1.1. Prevention Related to Parent Risk Factors

One important implication of the interactional model of child abuse is that violence in families can often be viewed as a consequence of a parent's lack of knowledge and lack of skill rather than the parent's inherent psychopathology. To the extent that certain parents harm their children because they lack information, skill, and competence for rearing children nonviolently, the incidence of maltreatment can be reduced by efforts that teach individuals appropriate, nonviolent methods of parenting and create a social value system favoring nonaggression toward children.

On a broad scale, primary prevention of child abuse should include greatly expanded attention to parenting issues in junior and senior high school curricula. Courses in secondary schools might include instruction in basic principles of child behavior and development, methods of child management, problems that are frequently encountered with children and ways that they can be appropriately handled, and alternatives to physical punishment. At present, few secondary schools present detailed information to students concerning these important issues; since most students will become parents and because an accepted mandate of education in this country is to prepare young people for successful living, educating students to child development issues and appropriate parenting skills stand out as neglected areas in most school curricula.

An advantage of planned, wide-scale attention to parenting matters in junior and senior high schools is that it can provide information to a broad population of future parents. Since individuals who will later become abusive parents are included in this larger population, information will reach them without requiring one to predict which particular student is likely to exhibit abusive behavior later. In more general fashion, well thought-out programs in child development and parenting skills can be of benefit to most other students, including those who simply have little practical knowledge about children. Thus, education programs of this type might serve two purposes: (1) providing corrective, remedial information to those in the student population who otherwise would experience serious difficulties with their children and are at risk of abuse, and (2) improving all students' level of knowledge about child development and appropriate parenting skills.

Unfortunately, there are several limitations to educational programs of this type. One is that they teach parenting skills to students at an age when many young people are not yet thinking of themselves as potential parents. Second, although mass educational programs can increase knowledge about children and appropriate parenting roles, it does not necessarily follow that information alone will make young people behaviorally skilled in handling their own children years later. For these reasons, it may also prove desirable to conduct intensive preventive educational programs for groups of people who are at higher risk for abuse or who are nearer the age of actually becoming parents.

This can be accomplished in a variety of ways. Because most parents give birth to children in hospitals and return to clinics or offices of some kind for postnatal care, parent education programs (including reading materials, videotape presentations, and child-care demonstrations), could be conducted while parents are in the hospital following the birth of their children, as well as when they return for postnatal care appointments. The use of videotape presentations that can be shown over closed-circuit television in maternity wards or in clinic waiting rooms may be particularly useful because they reach parents at a time when child-care topics should have both interest value and relevance.

If abused children are at a greater risk of later becoming abusive parents (a view widely asserted but not yet well substantiated through controlled, empirical studies), they would represent a group that clearly merits preventive intervention effort. As we discussed in Chapter 3, abused children have an observational learning and experience history that involve personal exposure to violent parenting models; they may also have special fears, uncertainities, or hostilities concerning parenthood as a result of their own childhood experiences. To date, there has been little systematic, longitudinal follow-up of abused children as they enter adolescence and later become parents themselves. However, it would seem especially relevant to follow previously abused children to assess whether they are likely to encounter problems as *they* become parents and to provide specialized preventive intervention for them. Since welfare authorities maintain archival records of abuse cases, it should be possible to identify previously abused children and to develop corrective educational and parent-training programs aimed at interrupting the intergenerational aspects of abuse. Before such efforts can be successful, empirical research is needed to better determine whether (and how) abused children are at risk of becoming abusive parents themselves.

Finally, to the extent that instances of child maltreatment can be traced to limited knowledge and skill in handling children, parents who are extremely young or inexperienced or who lack access to everyday sources of information on childrearing represent another higher-risk group that merits preventive intervention. Teenage parents and unmarried parents without a spouse to provide collaboration on everyday childrearing problems may especially benefit from educational and skills-training programs concerning parenting techniques.

10.1.2. Prevention Related to Child Factors

Although parents with serious child-management skill deficits may be unable to handle even routine behavior problems of their children or may label normal child behavior as problematic for them, it is reasonable to assume that children who *are* difficult to manage will be at even greater risk for physical maltreatment. As we saw in Chapter 2, the prevalance of behavior disorders and characteristics such as "hyperactivity" and "irritability" appears to be higher among abused children than nonabused children (Baldwin & Oliver, 1975; Friedrich & Boriskin, 1976; Helfer, 1973; Johnson & Morse, 1968; Milow & Lourie, 1964). If physically violent actions can occur because effective handling of a child's behavior requires skill which the parent lacks, those children who *do* require unusually skilled parenting probably frustrate, anger, and tax their parents more than other children. In essence, this means that "difficult" children are at greater risk for excessive punishment and, potentially, abusive discipline. By better identifying these difficult-to-manage children and offering early assistance, it should be possible to intervene in families before harsh disciplinary patterns become established and severe. From this perspective, an element of child abuse prevention is providing early treatment intervention for families experiencing less extreme problems with their children.

Community mental health centers, child/family guidance centers, and similar community-based clinics all have the potential for reducing the incidence of child abuse by more effectively reaching families with child-related problems. To accomplish this, parents must be aware that if they are experiencing difficulties with their children, community mental health facilities will provide useful, affordable, nonstigmatizing services. Media and community awareness campaigns to inform the public, and especially parents, of available services may be especially important.

In related fashion, earlier referral of children and their families to child clinics by other professionals should result in the more expedient treatment of potentially abusive families. Rather than attempting only to identify children who have already been abused, the staffs of schools, pediatric clinics, daycare centers, Headstart programs, and other agencies should be alerted to any evidence that a parent is having serious difficulties with his or her child and make referrals to an appropriate community treatment resource. This, once again, is consistent with our formulation that abusive parents do not represent a distinct clinical population, and that episodes of child-directed violence can occur in many families who are experiencing serious management problems with their children.

Finally, the child abuse literature suggests that certain infant and child characteristics other than management problems occur disproportionately more often in maltreating families and may thereby constitute child risk factors. Investigators have suggested that prematurity of birth (Elmer & Gregg, 1967; Fontana, 1973; Friedrich & Boriskin, 1976; McRae *et al.*, 1973), being an unwanted and unplanned infant (Johnson & Morse, 1968; Nurse, 1964; Smith *et al.*, 1974), or having a physical appearance or temperamental characteristics that are simply disliked by the parent (Green *et al.*, 1974) can all increase the likelihood of maltreatment. Unfortunately, there has not yet been sufficient research to determine if these are salient predictive variables and, consequently, whether specific prevention programs targeted toward them will be effective on a large scale.

10.1.3. Prevention Related to Situational and Stress Risk Factors

Sociological and demographic analyses have shown that rates of reported child maltreatment are highest in geographic areas most affected by poverty and socioeconomic stress (Garbarino, 1976; Garbarino & Sherman, 1980; Gil, 1970). These data, by implication, suggest that the social, economic, and environmental effects of poverty create stress or life-style crises that increase the likelihood of intra-family violence. However, it is important to recognize that the accuracy in which child abuse cases are reported and detected may vary across geographical areas as well. Clearly, controlled study is needed to determine whether the incidence of child maltreatment *changes* in a *single* geographical area when socioeconomic stress levels increase or decrease: Does the rate of child abuse increase during periods of high unemployment in a community? When low-cost daycare is made available, does the incidence of child maltreatment become lower? Does the creation or loss of other community resources (such as neighborhood centers, welfare assistance programs, and subsidized housing) coincide with changes in child maltreatment patterns? Close demographic analysis of the relationship between various social-economic events occurring in a community and change in reported rates of child abuse should lead to a more specific understanding of the way external stresses influence family violence. This, in turn, will provide a better focus for prevention.

Based on the existing literature and on current theorizing about the manner in which situational and social stress factors may contribute to violence, one can tentatively outline several preventive strategies that merit closer attention:

1. *Provision of affordable child-care alternatives.* Especially for parents faced with overwhelming child-care responsibilities, the availability of low-cost daycare could reduce family stress and provide a respite from these responsibilities. Low-cost child care has been traditionally funded by government agencies, but cooperative programs operated by parents themselves might also be implemented on a community-wide basis.

2. *Development of closer social support networks within communities.* If parents and families have opportunities to meet, socialize with, and work on civic projects with their neighbors, the problems of social isolation, insularity, and noninvolvement in community affairs can also be reduced. Neighborhood community centers, churches, and schools can more actively seek the participation of community resi-

dents in a range of social, civic, recreational, and neighborhood improvement projects. Although poverty per se is difficult to address in a prevention program, the social disorganization and deterioration that often accompanies poverty can be reduced through the development of community social resources.

3. *Efforts to lessen socioeconomic family stressors such as unemployment, limited access to community services, and poor living conditions.* Large-scale social and economic problems such as these defy simple corrective solutions. However, as Gil (1975) points out, if child abuse is more prevalent among families who are stressed by joblessness, inadequate basic community services, and deteriorated living conditions, these socioeconomic problems will need to be considered in prevention programs. In this sense, efforts to enhance the quality of overall community living circumstances may result in reduced frustration, stress, and likelihood of family violence.

As we have seen, child abuse is determined by a number of different factors. Just as the treatment of an individual abusive family follows from a careful assessment of the antecedents of that family's violence, community prevention efforts must also take into account a number of different potential causes. As research leads to a delineation of factors, applied community interventions will be better able to reduce the incidence of child abuse in our society.

Appendixes

Appendix I. The Eyberg Child Behavior Inventory

Appendix II. Knowledge of Behavioral Principles as Applied to Children

Appendix III. Deep Muscle Relaxation Training Script

I

The Eyberg Child Behavior Inventory

Reprinted from Eyberg and Ross (1978) with permission of the authors and *Journal of Clinical Child Psychology*.

Below are a series of phrases that describe children's behavior; Please (1) circle the number describing how often the behavior *currently* occurs with your child, and (2) circle either "yes" or "no" to indicate whether the behavior is *currently a problem.*

	How often does this occur with your child?							Is this a problem for you?	
	Never	Seldom		Sometimes	Often		Always		
1. Dawdles in getting dressed	1	2	3	4	5	6	7	Yes	No
2. Dawdles or lingers at mealtime	1	2	3	4	5	6	7	Yes	No
3. Has poor table manners	1	2	3	4	5	6	7	Yes	No
4. Refuses to eat food presented	1	2	3	4	5	6	7	Yes	No
5. Refuses to do chores when asked	1	2	3	4	5	6	7	Yes	No
6. Slow in getting ready for bed	1	2	3	4	5	6	7	Yes	No
7. Refuses to go to bed on time	1	2	3	4	5	6	7	Yes	No
8. Does not obey house rules on his own	1	2	3	4	5	6	7	Yes	No
9. Refuses to obey until threatened with punishment	1	2	3	4	5	6	7	Yes	No

10. Acts defiant when told to do something	1	2	3	4	5	6	7	Yes	No
11. Argues with parents about rules	1	2	3	4	5	6	7	Yes	No
12. Gets angry when doesn't get his own way	1	2	3	4	5	6	7	Yes	No
13. Has temper tantrums	1	2	3	4	5	6	7	Yes	No
14. Sasses adults	1	2	3	4	5	6	7	Yes	No
15. Whines	1	2	3	4	5	6	7	Yes	No
16. Cries easily	1	2	3	4	5	6	7	Yes	No
17. Yells or screams	1	2	3	4	5	6	7	Yes	No
18. Hits parents	1	2	3	4	5	6	7	Yes	No
19. Destroys toys and other objects	1	2	3	4	5	6	7	Yes	No
20. Is careless with toys and other objects	1	2	3	4	5	6	7	Yes	No
21. Steals	1	2	3	4	5	6	7	Yes	No
22. Lies	1	2	3	4	5	6	7	Yes	No
23. Teases or provokes other children	1	2	3	4	5	6	7	Yes	No
24. Verbally fights with friends his own age	1	2	3	4	5	6	7	Yes	No

	How often does this occur with your child?							Is this a problem for you?	
	Never	Seldom		Sometimes	Often		Always		
25. Verbally fights with sisters and brothers	1	2	3	4	5	6	7	Yes	No
26. Physically fights with friends his own age	1	2	3	4	5	6	7	Yes	No
27. Physically fights with sisters and brothers	1	2	3	4	5	6	7	Yes	No
28. Constantly seeks attention	1	2	3	4	5	6	7	Yes	No
29. Interrupts	1	2	3	4	5	6	7	Yes	No
30. Is easily distracted	1	2	3	4	5	6	7	Yes	No
31. Has short-attention span	1	2	3	4	5	6	7	Yes	No
32. Fails to finish tasks or projects	1	2	3	4	5	6	7	Yes	No

33. Has difficulty entertaining himself alone	1	2	3	4	5	6	7	Yes	No
34. Has difficulty concentrating on one thing	1	2	3	4	5	6	7	Yes	No
35. Is overactive or restless	1	2	3	4	5	6	7	Yes	No
36. Wets the bed	1	2	3	4	5	6	7	Yes	No

Other problems

______________________	1	2	3	4	5	6	7	Yes	No
______________________	1	2	3	4	5	6	7	Yes	No
______________________	1	2	3	4	5	6	7	Yes	No
______________________	1	2	3	4	5	6	7	Yes	No
______________________	1	2	3	4	5	6	7	Yes	No
______________________	1	2	3	4	5	6	7	Yes	No

II

Knowledge of Behavioral Principles as Applied to Children

Directions

Please use pencil.

Read each question and each of its four possible answers. Sometimes more than one answer could be correct under certain circumstances; however, you should select the best answer or the answer that is most generally true. Completely fill in the square beside that answer with a pencil.

Example:

Probably the most important influence in a young child's life is his

- ☐ Toys
- ☐ Television
- ☐ Parents
- ☐ Friends

Please do not consult others while deciding how to answer the question.

Be sure to fill in only one square for each question.

Be sure to answer every question even if you must guess.

1. Desirable and undesirable behavior are most alike in that they are:
   - ☐ The result of emotions and feelings.
   - ☐ Habits and therefore difficult to change.
   - ☐ Ways the child expresses himself.
   - ☐ The result of learning.
2. Probably the most important idea to keep in mind when first changing behavior is:
   - ☐ To use both reward and punishment.
   - ☐ To reward every time the desired behavior occurs.

- ☐ To be flexible about whether or not you reward.
- ☐ To be sure the child understands why you want the behavior to change.

3. Most problem behavior in young children is probably:
   - ☐ A reaction to deeper emotional problems.
   - ☐ Due to lack of communication in the home.
   - ☐ Accidentally taught by the child's family.
   - ☐ Due to a stage which the child will outgrow.

4. A child begins to whine and cry when his parent explains why he can't go outside. How should the parent react?
   - ☐ Ask the child why going outside is so important to him.
   - ☐ Explain that it is a parent's right to make such decisions.
   - ☐ Explain again why he should not go outside.
   - ☐ Ignore the whining and crying.

5. Which of the following is most important for parents in controlling their child's behavior?
   - ☐ The rules the parents make about behavior.
   - ☐ The parents' understanding of the child's feelings.
   - ☐ The behaviors to which the parents attend.
   - ☐ Being strict, but also warm and gentle.

6. In changing a child's behavior a parent should try to use:
   - ☐ About one reward for every punishment.
   - ☐ About one reward for every five punishments.
   - ☐ About five rewards for every punishment.
   - ☐ Practically all rewards.

7. Which of the following is the least likely way for children to react to the person who punishes them?
   - ☐ The child will try to avoid the punisher.
   - ☐ The child will have admiration and respect for the punisher.
   - ☐ The child may copy the punisher's methods and do similar things to playmates.
   - ☐ The child will associate the punishment with the punisher.

8. Which of the following statements is most true?
   - ☐ People usually fully understand the reasons for their actions.

- ☐ People are often unaware of the reasons for their actions.
- ☐ People's actions are mostly based on logic.
- ☐ It is necessary to understand the reason for a person's behavior before trying to change the behavior.

9. If you are trying to teach a child to talk, you should first:
   - ☐ Reward the child after speaking a sentence.
   - ☐ Reward the child for saying a word.
   - ☐ Reward the child for any vocalization.
   - ☐ Punish the child if he did not speak.

10. If punishment is used for a behavior such as playing football in the house, which type is probably best to use?
    - ☐ Make the child do extra homework.
    - ☐ Clearly express your disapproval.
    - ☐ Remove the child to a boring situation each time.
    - ☐ A reasonable spanking.

11. A child has been rewarded each time he cleans his room. In order to keep the room clean without having to use a reward, the next step should probably be to:
    - ☐ Have a talk about how pleased you are and then stop giving the reward.
    - ☐ Give the reward about one out of five times.
    - ☐ Give the reward almost every time.
    - ☐ You must always reward it every time.

12. Parents who use lots of rewards for good behavior and few punishments will probably tend to have children who:
    - ☐ Do not understand discipline.
    - ☐ Will not cooperate unless they are "paid."
    - ☐ Take advantage of their parents.
    - ☐ Are well-behaved and cooperative.

13. When should a child who is just learning to dress himself be praised the first time?
    - ☐ When he gets his foot through the first hole in his underwear.
    - ☐ When he gets his underwear completely on.
    - ☐ When he asks to do it himself.
    - ☐ When he has completely finished dressing himself.

14. Which of the following is most effective in getting a child to do homework?
    - ☐ "When you finish your homework, you can watch T.V."
    - ☐ "You can watch this show on T.V. if you promise to do your homework when the show is over."
    - ☐ "If you don't do your homework tonight, you can't watch T.V. at all tomorrow."
    - ☐ Explain the importance of school work and the dangers of putting things off.

15. Three of the following responses refer to forms of punishment which are mild and effective. Which one is not?
    - ☐ Ignoring the undesirable behavior.
    - ☐ Sending the child to a dull room for a few minutes.
    - ☐ Taking away something the child likes (such as dessert after supper).
    - ☐ Scolding.

16. Each time Mother starts to read, Billy begins making a lot of noise which prevents her from enjoying her reading time. The best way for Mother to get Billy to be quiet while she reads is to:
    - ☐ Severely reprimand him when this occurs.
    - ☐ Pay close attention and praise and hug him when he plays quietly while she is reading and ignore his noisy behavior.
    - ☐ Call him to her and explain carefully how important it is for her to have a quiet time for herself each time this occurs.
    - ☐ Tell him that he won't get a dessert after dinner if he continues.

17. Which of the following is the most effective form of punishment in the long run for reducing a child's undesirable behavior?
    - ☐ Scolding him every time he does it.
    - ☐ Occasionally spanking him when he does it.
    - ☐ Sending him to his room for five minutes every time he does it.
    - ☐ Sending him to his room all afternoon every time he does it.

18. A young child often whines and cries when he is around his mother. In trying to find out why he cries, his mother should probably first consider the possibility that:
    - ☐ He is trying to tell her something.

- ☐ He needs more of her attention.
- ☐ She is somehow rewarding his crying.
- ☐ She is not giving him enough attention.

19. A good rule to remember is:
    - ☐ Do not reward with money if possible.
    - ☐ Catch a child doing something right.
    - ☐ Reward good behavior and always punish bad behavior.
    - ☐ Punishment is always unnecessary.

20. If a child very gradually receives rewards less and less often for a behavior, what is most likely to happen?
    - ☐ He will soon stop the behavior.
    - ☐ He will be more likely to behave that way for a long time.
    - ☐ He will not trust the person giving the rewards.
    - ☐ None of the above.

21. Which of the following is true about punishment?
    - ☐ Punishment teaches respect.
    - ☐ Punishment should be delayed until it can be carefully determined that it is really necessary.
    - ☐ Punishment can teach a child new behaviors.
    - ☐ Some punishments can result in a child becoming aggressive.

22. In a reading group, the teacher gives each child candy plus praise for each correct answer. Which of the following statements is most true?
    - ☐ The candy is a bribe and doesn't belong in a school setting.
    - ☐ At first, the children work to earn the candy and may later work for the praise alone.
    - ☐ Children shouldn't be "paid" for doing their school work.
    - ☐ It probably doesn't make much difference whether or not candy is used because the children who want to learn to read will do so and the others won't.

23. A boy loves football. What is most likely to happen if, each time he is playing nicely with his sister, his father invites him to play football?
    - ☐ He will always be asking his father to play football.
    - ☐ He will play nicely with his sister more often.

- ☐ He will be annoyed with his father for interfering with his activities.
- ☐ He will be encouraged to teach his sister to play football.

24. To record, graph and note the direction of the change of a behavior is:
    - ☐ A minor, optional step in a behavior-change program.
    - ☐ An important step in a behavior-change program.
    - ☐ A procedure employed only by scientists for research.
    - ☐ Time consuming and complicated. Therefore, these procedures should only be used in special cases.

25. A father is teaching his son to hit a thrown ball with a bat. Which of the following methods will probably most help his son to learn to hit?
    - ☐ Let him try to hit the ball without saying anything, so the child can learn on his own.
    - ☐ Occasionally tell him what he is doing wrong.
    - ☐ Occasionally tell him what he is doing right.
    - ☐ Tell him almost every time he does something right.

26. Which of the following is most true about physical punishment?
    - ☐ It should immediately follow the undesirable behavior and at full intensity.
    - ☐ It should be mild and immediately follow the undesirable behavior.
    - ☐ It should begin in a mild form and, if that doesn't work, intensity should gradually be increased.
    - ☐ It is ineffective and inappropriate.

27. Punishment, as a way to get rid of an undesirable behavior, is best used when:
    - ☐ You are very upset.
    - ☐ You want to teach the child the right way to behave.
    - ☐ The behavior may be dangerous.
    - ☐ Scolding doesn't seem to be effective.

28. Which of the following is not an important step in a behavior-change program?
    - ☐ Make certain the child feels ashamed for his misbehavior.

- ☐ Decide on a particular behavior that you wish to change.
- ☐ If necessary, break the selected behavior down into smaller steps.
- ☐ Select a proper time and situation for measuring the behavior.

29. If you want your child to develop proper study habits, you should:
    - ☐ Encourage him to do his homework.
    - ☐ Help him to see school as pleasant.
    - ☐ Reward him whenever he studies.
    - ☐ Give him good reasons why he will need school.

30. Two brothers fight constantly. Their parents decide to praise them when they play together nicely. However, they still continue to fight. Punishment may be necessary. What is probably happening?
    - ☐ They don't want their parents' praise.
    - ☐ The benefits of fighting are stronger to them than their parents' praise.
    - ☐ They have too much anger toward each other to control.
    - ☐ They are at a stage they will grow out of.

31. A child often cries over any small matter that bothers her. How should her parents react to best reduce her crying?
    - ☐ Reward when she reacts without crying.
    - ☐ Use a mild punishment when she cries.
    - ☐ Try to find out what is really troubling the child and deal with that.
    - ☐ Provide her with something interesting so she will stop crying.

32. Mrs. Thomas found out that spanking her seven-year-old son, Bob, did not seem to stop him from using "naughty" words. A friend suggested that rather than spanking him, she should send him to be by himself. The room he is sent to should be:
    - ☐ His own room, so he will still have something to do.
    - ☐ Small and dark.
    - ☐ As uninteresting as possible.
    - ☐ A large room.

33. If you want your child to say "please" and "thank you" at the table, it is probably most important to:
    - ☐ Reprimand him when he forgets to say them.
    - ☐ Explain why good manners are important.

- ☐ Remember to compliment him when he remembers to say them.
- ☐ Praise other members of the family when they use these words.

34. Which reward is probably best to help a 12-year-old child improve his arithmetic skills?
    - ☐ A dollar for each evening he studies.
    - ☐ A dime for each problem he works correctly.
    - ☐ Ten dollars for each A he receives on his report card in arithmetic.
    - ☐ A bicycle for passing arithmetic for the rest of the year.

35. A major problem has been getting Leon to bed in the evening. His mother has decided to change this and wants to measure the relevant behaviors. Which is the best way for her to do this?
    - ☐ Each evening, record whether or not he goes to bed on time.
    - ☐ Chart his behavior all day long, up to and including bedtime to try to find out what causes his not wanting to go to bed.
    - ☐ Each week, make a note of how easy or difficult it has been to get him to bed.
    - ☐ Ask Leon to keep his own record each week.

36. Mr. Jones agreed to pay his son, Mike, 25¢ each time he carries out the trash. If Mr. Jones forgets to give Mike the money for a few days, what is most likely to happen?
    - ☐ Mike will continue to take out the trash because he realizes how important this is.
    - ☐ Mike will stop taking out the trash.
    - ☐ Mike will begin to do extra chores, as well as take out the trash, so his father will notice how well he's doing and remember to give Mike the money.
    - ☐ Mike will start to misbehave to take out his anger about not being paid.

37. A father tells a child she cannot go to the store with him because she didn't clean her room like she promised. She reacts by shouting, crying and promising she will clean the room when she gets home. What should the father do?
    - ☐ Ignore her and go to the store.

☐ Take her to the store but make her clean her room when they return.
☐ Calm her down and go help her clean her room.
☐ Talk to her and find out why she doesn't take responsibility.

38. The first step in changing a problem behavior is to:
☐ Reward the child when he is behaving nicely.
☐ Punish the child for misbehavior.
☐ Carefully observe the behavior.
☐ Seek help from someone who is more objective.

39. In changing a behavior it is most important to use:
☐ Methods which have been tested by others.
☐ Consequences which are rewarding to the child.
☐ Consequences which are punitive to the child.
☐ Rewards which do not bribe the child.

40. Johnny has just torn up a new magazine. Of the following choices, which is the best way for his mother to discipline him?
☐ Tell him he will be spanked by his father when he gets home.
☐ Punish him then and there.
☐ Explain to Johnny about the wrongness of his action.
☐ Angrily scold Johnny so that he will learn that such an act is bad and upsetting to his mother.

41. Stan is doing a number of things that greatly disturb his parents. It would be best for them to:
☐ Try to eliminate quickly all of these undesirable behaviors at once.
☐ Select just a few behaviors to deal with at first.
☐ Select the single behavior they find most disruptive and concentrate on changing that.
☐ Wait for 28–30 days before beginning to try to change his behaviors to make certain they are stable and persistent.

42. Which would be the best example of an appropriate way to praise Mary?
☐ Good girl, Mary.
☐ I love you, Mary.

- ☐ I like the way you helped me put the dishes away.
- ☐ I'll tell your father how nice you were when he comes home.

43. Listed below are four methods used to change behavior. Which is usually the best technique to get Frank to stop sucking his thumb?
    - ☐ Punish the undesired behavior.
    - ☐ Ignore the behavior.
    - ☐ Reward him for desirable behavior in the situation in which he usually misbehaves.
    - ☐ Explain to the child why the behavior is undesirable.

44. Jimmy sometimes says obscene words, but only in front of his mother. She has been shocked and makes her feelings clear to him. How should she react when he uses obscene words?
    - ☐ Wash his mouth out with soap.
    - ☐ Ignore him when he uses obscene words.
    - ☐ Tell him how bad he is and how she doesn't like him when he uses those words.
    - ☐ Explain to him the reason such words are not used.

45. If you want to make a behavior a long-lasting habit, you should:
    - ☐ Reward it every time.
    - ☐ First reward it every time and then reward it occasionally.
    - ☐ Promise something the child wants very much.
    - ☐ Give several reasons why it is important and remind the child of the reasons often.

46. Punishment will not be effective unless you:
    - ☐ Prevent the child from escaping while you punish him.
    - ☐ Throw all of your emotions into the punishment.
    - ☐ Follow it with a careful explanation of your reasons for the punishment.
    - ☐ Have tried everything else.

47. The most likely reason a child misbehaves is because:
    - ☐ He is expressing angry feelings which he often holds inside.
    - ☐ He has learned to misbehave.
    - ☐ He was born with a tendency to misbehave.
    - ☐ He has not been properly told that his behavior is wrong.

48. Which of the following is probably most important in helping a child behave in desirable ways?
    - ☐ To teach him the importance of self-discipline.
    - ☐ To help him understand right and wrong.
    - ☐ Providing consistent consequences for his behavior.
    - ☐ Understanding his moods and feelings as a unique person.

49. A baby often screams for several minutes and gets his parents' attention. Which of the following is probably the best way for his parents to reduce his screaming?
    - ☐ If there is nothing physically wrong with the child, ignore his screaming even though the first few times he screams even louder.
    - ☐ Distract the child with something he finds interesting whenever he screams.
    - ☐ Ignore all noises and sounds the child makes.
    - ☐ None of the above. Babies usually have good reasons for screaming.

50. How often a behavior occurs is probably mostly controlled by:
    - ☐ The person's attitude about his behavior.
    - ☐ What happens to him at the same time the behavior occurs.
    - ☐ What happens to him just before the behavior occurs.
    - ☐ What happens to him just after the behavior occurs.

KEY:					
	1. d	12. d	23. b	34. b	45. b
	2. b	13. a	24. b	35. a	46. a
	3. c	14. a	25. d	36. b	47. b
	4. d	15. d	26. a	37. a	48. c
	5. c	16. b	27. c	38. c	49. a
	6. d	17. c	28. a	39. b	50. d
	7. b	18. c	29. c	40. b	
	8. b	19. b	30. b	41. c	
	9. c	20. b	31. a	42. c	
	10. c	21. d	32. c	43. c	
	11. c	22. b	33. c	44. b	

III

Deep Muscle Relaxation Training Script

Now, settle back as comfortably as you can, close your eyes, and listen to what I'm going to tell you. I'm going to make you aware of certain sensations in your body and then show you how you can reduce these sensations. First direct your attention to your left arm, your left hand in particular. Clench your left fist. Clench it tightly and study the tension in the hand and in the forearm. Study those sensations of tension. And now let go. Relax the left hand and let it rest on the arm of the chair. And note the difference between the tension and the relaxation. (10-second pause.) Once again now, clench your left hand into a fist, tightly, noticing the tensions in the hand and in the forearm. Study those tensions, and now let go. Let your fingers spread out, relaxed, and note the difference once again between muscular tension and muscular relaxation. (10-second pause.)

Now let's do the same with the right hand. Clench the right fist. Study those tensions (5-second pause) and now relax. Relax the right fist. Note the difference once again between the tension and the relaxation. And enjoy the contrast (10-second pause.) Once again now, clench the right fist, clench it tight. Study the tensions. Study them. And now relax the right fist. Let the fingers spread out comfortably. See if you can keep letting go a little bit more. Even though it seems as if you've let go as much as you possibly can, there always seems to be that extra bit of relaxation. Note the difference once again between the tension and the relaxation. Note the looseness beginning to develop in the left and right arms and hands. Both your left and right arms and hands now are a little bit more relaxed.

Now bend both hands back at the wrists so that you tense the muscles in the back of the hand and in the forearm. Fingers pointing toward the ceiling. Study the tension, and now relax. Let your hands return to their resting positions, and note the difference between tension and relaxation. (10-second pause.) Do that once again—fingers pointing to the ceiling, feeling that tension in the backs of the hands and in the forearms. And now relax. Let go. Further and further. (10-second pause.)

Now clench both your hands into fists and bring them toward your shoulders so as to tighten your biceps muscles, the large muscles in the upper part of the arm. Feel the tension in the biceps muscles. And now relax. Let your arms drop down again to your sides, and note the difference between the tension that was in your biceps and the relative relaxation you feel now. (10-second pause.) Let's do that once again now. Clench both biceps muscles, bringing both arms up, trying to touch with your fists the respective shoulders. Study that tension. Hold it, study it. And now relax. Once again, let the arms drop and study the feelings of relaxation, the contrast between tension and relaxation. Just keep letting go of those muscles, further and further. (10-second pause.)

Now we can direct our attention to the shoulder area. Shrug your shoulders, bringing both shoulders up toward your ears, as if you wanted to touch your ears with your shoulders. And note the tension in your shoulders and up in your neck. Study that tension. Hold it. And now relax. Let both shoulders return to a resting position. Just keep letting go, further and further. Once again, note the contrast between the tension and the relaxation that's now spreading into your shoulder areas. (10-second pause.) Do that once again. Bring both shoulders up as if to touch the ears. Feel the tension in the shoulders, in the upper back, in the neck. Study the tension in these muscles. And now relax. Loosen those muscles. Let your shoulders come down to a resting position, and study the contrast once again between the tension and relaxation. (10-second pause.)

You can also learn to relax more completely the various muscles of the face. So, what I want you to do now is to wrinkle up your forehead and brow. Wrinkle it until you feel all your forehead very much wrinkled, the muscles tense, and skin furrowed. And now relax. Smooth out the forehead. Let those muscles become loose. (10-second pause.) Do that once again. Wrinkle up your forehead. Study those tensions in the muscles above the eyes, in the forehead region. And now, smooth out your forehead. Relax those muscles. And once again note the contrast between the tension and the relaxation. (10-second pause.)

Now close your eyes very tightly. Close them tightly so that you can feel tension all around your eyes and the many muscles that control the movements of the eyes. (5-second pause.) And now relax those muscles, let them relax, noting the difference between the tension and the relaxation. (10-second pause.) Do that once again now. Eyes tightly closed and study the tension. Hold it. (5-second pause.) And relax, let go, and let your eyes remain comfortably closed. (10-second pause.)

Now clench your jaws, bite your teeth together. Study the tension throughout the jaws. (5-second pause.) Relax your jaws now. Let your lips part slightly, and note the difference between tension and relaxation in your jaw area. (10-second pause.) Once again, jaws clenched. Study the tension. (5-second pause.) And now let go, further and further. Just continue to relax. (10-second pause.)

Now purse your lips, press your lips together. That's right, press them together very tightly and feel the tension all around the mouth. And now relax, relax those muscles around the mouth, and just let your chin rest comfortably. Once again now, press your lips together and study the tension around the mouth. Hold it (5-second pause.) And now relax. Let go of those muscles, more and more, further and further. (10-second pause.) Note how much looser the various muscles have perhaps become in those parts of the body that we have successively tensed and relaxed; your hands, forearms, upper arms, your shoulders, the various facial muscles.

And now we'll turn our attention to the neck. Press your head back against the surface on which it's resting. Press it back so that you can feel the tension, primarily in the back of the neck and in the upper back. Hold it, study it. And now let go, let your head rest comfortably now, and enjoy the contrast between the tension you created before, and the greater relaxation you can feel now. Just keep letting go, further and further, more and more, to the best of your ability. Do that once again, head pressed back, study the tension, hold it, (5-second pause) and now let go, just relax, let go, further and further. (10-second pause.)

Now I'd like you to bring your head forward, and try to bury your chin into your chest. Feel the tension, especially in the front of your neck. And now relax, let go, further and further. (10-second pause.) Do that once again now. Chin buried in the chest, hold it. (5-second pause.) And now relax, just relax, further and further. (10-second pause.)

Now we can direct our attention to the muscles of the upper back. Arch your back, arch it, sticking out your chest and stomach so that you feel tension in your back, primarily in your upper back. Study that tension and now relax. Let the body once again rest against the back of the chair or the bed, and note the difference between the tension and the relaxation, letting those muscles get looser and looser. (10-second pause.) Once again now arch the back way up. Study the tensions. Hold it. (5-second pause.) And now relax the back once again, letting go of all the tensions in these muscles. (10-second pause.)

And now take a deep breath, fill your lungs, and hold it. Hold it and study the tension all through your chest and down into your stomach area. Study that tension, and now relax, let go. Exhale and continue breathing as you were. Note once again the difference between the tension and the relaxation. (10-second pause.) Let's do that once again. Take a deep breath and hold it. Hold it. Study those tensions. Study them. Note the muscles tensing. Note the sensations. And now exhale and continue breathing as you were, very comfortably breathing, letting those muscles of the chest and some of the stomach muscles relax, getting more and more relaxed, each time you exhale. (10-second pause.)

And now tighten up the muscles in your stomach. Tense those stomach muscles. Hold it. Make the stomach very hard. And now relax. Let those muscles become loose. Just let go and relax. (10-second pause.) Do that once again. Tighten those stomach muscles. Study the tension. (5-second pause.) And now relax, let go, further and further, more and more. Loosen the tensions. Get rid of the tensions and note the contrast between tension and relaxation. (10-second pause.)

I'd like you now to stretch both legs. Stretch them so that you can feel tension in the thighs. Stretch them way out, (5-second pause) and now relax. Let them relax and note the difference once again between tension in the thigh muscles and the relative relaxation you can feel now. (10-second pause.) Do that once again, locking your knees, stretch out both legs so that you can feel the muscles of your thighs getting very hard, very tense. (5-second pause.) And now relax, relax those muscles. Let them get loose. Get rid of all tensions in the muscles of your thighs. (10-second pause.)

Now tense both calf muscles by pointing your toes toward your head. If you point your toes upward toward your head, you can feel the pulling, the tension, the contraction in your calf muscles and in your shins as well. Study that tension. And now relax. Let the legs relax and note once again the difference between tension and relaxation. (10-second pause.) Once again now, bend your feet back at the ankles, toes pointing toward your head, and study the tension. Hold it, study it. And now let go, relax those muscles, further and further, more and more deeply relaxed. (10-second pause.)

Just as you have been directing your muscles to tense you've also been directing them to relax or to loosen. You've noted the difference between tension and muscular relaxation. You can notice whether there is any tension in your muscles, and if there is, you can try to concentrate on that part, send messages to that muscle to loosen, to relax. If you think of loosening that muscle, you will in fact be able to do so, even if only a little.

Now, as you sit there in the chair, I'm going to review the various muscle groups that we've covered. As I name each group, try to notice if there is any tension in those muscles. If there is any, try to concentrate on those muscles and send messages to them to relax, to loosen. (5-second pause.) Relax the muscles in your feet, ankles, and calves. (5-second pause.) Shins, knees, and thighs. (5-second pause) Buttocks and hips. (5-second pause.) Loosen the muscles of your lower body. (5-second pause.) Relax your stomach, waist, lower back. (5-second pause.) Upper back, chest, and shoulders. (5-second pause.) Relax your upper arms, forearms, and hands, right to the tips of your fingers. (5-second pause.) Let the muscles of your throat and neck loosen. (5-second pause.) Relax your jaw and facial muscles. (5-second pause.) Let all the muscles of your body become loose. (5-second pause.) Now sit quietly with your eyes closed. (5-second pause.) Do nothing more than that. Just sit quietly with your eyes closed for a few minutes. (2-minute pause.)

References

Alvy, K. T. Preventing child abuse. *American Psychologist,* 1975, *30,* 921–928.

Arkowitz, H. Measurement and modifications of minimal dating behavior. In M. Hersen, R. Eisler, & P. Miller (Eds.), *Progress in behavior modification* (Vol. 5). New York: Academic Press, 1977.

Aronfreed, J. *Conduct and conscience.* New York: Academic Press, 1968.

Azrin, N. H. Some effects of noise on human behavior. *Journal of the Experimental Analysis of Behavior,* 1958, *1,* 183–200.

Azrin, N. H., Flores, T., & Kaplan, S. J. Job-finding club: A group-assisted program for obtaining employment. *Behavior Research and Therapy,* 1975, *13,* 17–27.

Azrin, N. H., Holz, W. C., & Hake, D. F. Fixed ratio punishment. *Journal of the Experimental Analysis of Behavior,* 1963, *6,* 141–148.

Baldwin, J. A. & Oliver, J. R. Epidemiology and family characteristics of severely abused children. *British Journal of Preventive Medicine,* 1975, *29,* 205–221.

Bandura, A. *Aggression: A social learning analysis.* Englewood Cliffs, NJ: Prentice-Hall, 1973.

Bandura, A. & Walters, R. H. *Social learning and personality development.* New York: Holt, Rinehart, and Winston, 1963.

Becker, W. C. *Parents are teachers.* Champaign, IL: Research Press, 1971.

Bell, G. Parents who abuse their children. *Canadian Psychiatric Association Journal,* 1973, *18,* 223–228.

Bell, R. An interpretation of the direction of effects in studies of socialization. *Psychological Review,* 1968, *75,* 81–95.

Belsky, J. Three theoretical models of child abuse: A critical review. *Child Abuse and Neglect,* 1978, *2,* 37–49.

Bennie, E. H. & Sclare, A. B. The battered child syndrome. *American Journal of Psychiatry,* 1969, *125,* 975–979.

Benoit, R. B. & Mayer, G. R. Time out: Guidelines for its selection and use. *The Personnel and Guidance Journal,* 1975, *53,* 501–506.

Berger, A. M. The child abusing family: II. Child and child rearing variables, environmental factors and typologies of abusing families. *American Journal of Family Therapy*, 1980, *8*, 53–66.

Berkowitz, E. Some determinants of impulsive aggression: Role of mediated associations with reinforcement for aggression. *Psychological Review*, 1974, *81*, 165–176.

Berkowitz, L. *Aggression: A social psychological analysis*. New York: McGraw-Hill, 1962.

Bernhardt, A. J. & Forehand, R. The effects of labeled and unlabeled praise upon lower and middle class children. *Journal of Experimental Child Psychology*, 1975, *19*, 536–543.

Bernstein, D. A. & Borkovec, T. D. *Progressive relaxation training: A manual for the helping professions*. Champaign, IL: Research Press, 1973.

Blanchard, E. B. & Ahles, L. A. Behavioral treatment of psychophysical disorders. *Behavior Modification*, 1979, *3*, 518–549.

Blumberg, M. L. Psychopathology of the abusing parent. *American Journal of Psychotherapy*, 1974, *28*, 21–29.

Boisvert, M. J. The battered child syndrome. *Social Casework*, 1972, *53*, 475–480.

Borkovec, T. D., & Sides, J. K. Critical procedural variables related to the physiological effects of progressive relaxation: A review. *Behavior Research and Therapy*, 1979, *17*, 119–125.

Bostow, D. E. & Bailey, J. Modifications of severe disruptive and aggressive behavior using brief timeout and reinforcement procedures. *Journal of Applied Behavior Analysis*, 1969, *2*, 21–38.

Brown, R. *Social psychology*. New York: The Free Press, 1965.

Burgess, R. L. & Conger, R. D. Family interaction in abusive, neglectful and normal families. *Child Development*, 1978, *49*, 1163–1173.

Burgess, R. L. Child abuse: A situational analysis. In B. B. Lahey & A. E. Kazdin (Eds.), *Advances in clinical child psychology* (Vol. 2). New York: Plenum Press, 1979.

Burgess, R. L. & Conger, R. D. Differentiating abusing and neglecting parents by direct observation of parent–child interaction. In M. L. Lauderdale, R. N. Anderson & S. E. Cramer (Eds.), *Child abuse and neglect: Issues on innovation and implementation. Proceedings of the Second Annual National Conference on Child Abuse and Neglect* (Vol. I). Washington, DC: U.S. Government Printing Office, 1977 (DHEW Publication No. (OHDS)78-30147). (a)

Burgess, R. L. & Conger, R. D. Family interaction patterns related to child abuse and neglect: Some preliminary findings. *Child Abuse and Neglect*, 1977, *1*, 269–277. (b)

Carlson, C. S., Arnold, C. R., Becker, W. C., & Madsen, G. H. The elimination of tantrum behavior of a child in an elementary school classroom. *Behavior Research and Therapy*, 1968, *6*, 117–120.

Cochrane, W. The battered child syndrome. *Canadian Journal of Public Health*, 1965, *56*, 193–196.

Cohen, B. M. & Etheridge, J. M. Recruiting's main ingredient. *Journal of College Placement*, 1975, *35*, 75–77.

Cohen, S. J. & Sussman, A. The incidence of child abuse in the United States. *Child Welfare*, 1975, *55*, 432–443.

Crimmins, D., Bradlyn, A. S., St. Lawrence, J. S., & Kelly, J. A. In-clinic training to improve the parent–child interaction skills of a neglectful mother. Unpublished manuscript, University of Mississippi Medical Center, 1982.

Crozier, J. & Katz, R. C. Social learning treatment of child abuse. *Journal of Behavior Therapy and Experimental Psychiatry*, 1979, *10*, 213–220.

Curran, J. P. Skills training as an approach to the treatment of heterosexual-social anxiety. *Psychological Bulletin*, 1977, *84*, 140–157.

Delsordo, J. D. Protective casework for abused children. *Children*, 1963, *10*, 213–218.

Denicola, J. & Sandler, J. Training child abusive parents in child management and self-control skills. *Behavior Therapy*, 1980, *11*, 263–270.

Disbrow, M. A., Doerr, H., & Caulfield, C. Measuring the components of parents' potential for child abuse and neglect. *Child Abuse and Neglect*, 1977, *1*, 279–296.

Doctor, R. M. & Singer, E. M. Behavioral intervention strategies with child abusive parents. *Child Abuse and Neglect*, 1978, *2*, 57–68.

Dollard, J., Doob, L., Miller, N., Mowrer, O. H., & Sears, P. R. *Frustration and aggression*. New Haven: Yale University Press, 1939.

Drake, L. T., Kaplan, H. R., & Stone, R. A. How do employers value the interview? *Journal of College Placement*, 1975, *32*, 47–51.

Dubanowski, R. A., Evans, I. M., & Higuchi, A. A. Analysis and treatment of child abuse: A set of behavioral propositions. *Child Abuse and Neglect*, 1978, *2*, 153–172.

D'Zurilla, T. J. & Goldfried, M. R. Problem solving and behavior modification. *Journal of Abnormal Psychology*, 1971, *78*, 107–126.

Ebbin, A. J., Gollub, M. H., Stein, A. M., & Wilson, M. G. Battered child syndrome at the Los Angeles County General Hospital. *American Journal of Diseases of Children*, 1969, *118*, 660–667.

The Education Commission of the States. *Child abuse and neglect: Alternatives for state legislation*, 6 (Report No. 44, 1973).

Ellis, A. *Humanistic psychology: The rational-emotive approach*. New York: Julian Press, 1973.

Ellis, A. *How to live with and without anger*. New York: Readers Digest Press, 1977.

Elmer, E. *Fragile families, troubled children*. Pittsburgh: University of Pittsburgh Press, 1977.

Elmer, E. & Gregg, G. S. Developmental characteristics of abused children. *Pediatrics*, 1967, *40*, 596–602.

Eyberg, S. M. & Ross, A. W. Assessment of child behavior problems: The validation of a new inventory. *Journal of Clinical Child Psychology*, 1978, *7*, 113–116.

Felsenthal, N. *Orientations to mass communication*. Chicago: Science Research Associates, 1976.

Festinger, L. *A theory of cognitive dissonance*. New York: Row, Peterson, 1957.

Floyd, L. M. Personality characteristics of abusing and neglecting mothers. Unpublished dissertation, Louisiana State University, 1975.

Fontana, V. J. *The maltreated child: The maltreatment syndrome in children*. Springfield, IL: Charles C Thomas, 1964.

Fontana, V. J. Further reflections on maltreatment of children. *Pediatrics*, 1973, *51*, 780–782.

Forehand, R. L. & McMahon, R. J. *Helping the noncompliant child: A clinician's guide to parent training*. New York: Guilford Press, 1981.

Fox, L. The home visitation program: An approach to positive mothering. *Child Abuse and Neglect*, 1977, *1*, 397–401.

Fraser, B. G. The child and his parents: A delicate balance of rights. In R. E. Helfer & C. H. Kempe (Eds.), *Child abuse and neglect*. Cambridge, MA: Ballinger, 1976.

Frazier, J. R. & Schneider, H. Parental management of inappropriate hyperactivity in a young retarded child. *Journal of Behavior Therapy and Experimental Psychiatry*, 1975, *6*, 246–247.

Friedman, R. M., Sandler, J., Hernandez, M., & Wolfe, D. A. Child abuse. In E. J. Mash & L. G. Terdal (Eds.), *Behavioral assessment of childhood disorders*. New York: Guilford Press, 1981.

Friedman, S. B. & Morse, C. W. Child abuse: A five-year follow-up of early case finding in the emergency department. *Pediatrics*, 1974, *54*, 404–410.

Friedrich, W. N. & Boriskin, S. A. The role of the child in abuse: A review of the literature. *American Journal of Orthopsychiatry*, 1976, *46*, 580–590.

Frodi, A. & Lamb, M. E. Child abusers' responses to infant smiles and cries. *Child Development*, 1980, *51*, 238–241.

Gaines, R., Sandgrund, A., Green, A. H., & Power, E. Etiological factors in child maltreatment: A multivariate study of abusing, neglecting, and normal mothers. *Journal of Abnormal Psychology*, 1978, *87*, 531–540.

Galassi, J. P., Galassi, M. D., & Litz, M. D. Assertive training in groups using video feedback. *Journal of Counseling Psychology*, 1974, *21*, 390–394.

Galdston, R. Observations on children who have been physically abused and their parents. *American Journal of Psychiatry*, 1965, *122*, 440–443.

Garbarino, J. A preliminary study of some ecological correlates of child abuse: The impact of socioeconomic stress on mothers. *Child Development*, 1976, *47*, 178–185.

Garbarino, J. & Sherman, D. High risk neighborhoods and high risk families: The human ecology of child maltreatment. *Child Development*, 1980, *51*, 188–198.

Geismar, L. L. *Preventive intervention in social work*. Metuchen, NJ: Scarecrow Press, 1969.

Gelles, R. J. Child abuse as psychopathology: A sociological critique and reformulation. *American Journal of Orthopsychiatry*, 1973, *43*, 611–621.

Gelles, R. J. Violence toward children in the United States. *American Journal of Orthopsychiatry*, 1978, *48*, 580–592.

Gil, D. G. A sociocultural perspective on physical child abuse. *Child Welfare*, 1971, *50*, 389–395.

Gil, D. G. *Violence against children: Physical child abuse in the United States*. Cambridge, MA: Harvard University Press, 1970.

Gil, D. G. Unraveling child abuse. *American Journal of Orthopsychiatry*, 1975, *45*, 346–356.

Giovannoni, J. M. Parental mistreatment: Perpetrators and victims. *Journal of Marriage and the Family*, 1971, *33*, 649–657.

Giovannoni, J. & Billingsley, A. Child neglect among the poor: A study of parental inadequacy in families of three ethnic groups. *Child Welfare*, 1970, *49*, 196–204.

Goldfried, M. R. & Davison, G. C. *Clinical behavior therapy*. New York: Holt, Rinehart & Winston, 1976.

Green, A. H. A psychodynamic approach to the study and treatment of child-abusing parents. *Journal of the Academy of Child Psychiatry*, 1976, *15*, 414–429.

Green, A. H., Gaines, R. W., & Sandgrund, A. Child abuse: Pathological syndrome of family interaction. *American Journal of Psychiatry*, 1974, *131*, 882–886.

Hall, R. V., Axelrod, S., Tyler, L., Grief, E., Jones, F. C., & Robertson, R. Modification of behavior problems in the home with the parent as observer and experimenter. *Journal of Applied Behavior Analysis*, 1972, *5*, 53–64.

Heimberg, R. G., Madsen, C. H., Montgomery, D., & McNabb, C. E. Behavioral treatments for heterosocial problems: Effects on daily self-monitored and role-played interactions. *Behavior Modification*, 1980, *4*, 147–172.

Helfer, R. E. & Kempe, C. H. (Eds.), *Child abuse and neglect: The family and the community*. Cambridge, MA: Ballinger, 1976.

Helfer, R. E., Schneider, C., & Hoffmeister, J. K. *Manual for use of the Michigan Screening Profile of Parenting*. East Lansing: Michigan State University Press, 1977.

Helfer, R. E. The etiology of child abuse. *Pediatrics*, 1973, *51*, 777.

Hersen, M., Eisler, R. M., & Miller, P. M. Development of assertive responses: Clinical, measurement, and research considerations. *Behaviour Research and Therapy*, 1973, *11*, 505–521.

Hillenberg, J. B., & Collins, F. C. A procedural analysis and review of relaxation training research. *Behavior Research and Therapy*, 1982, *20*, 251–260.

Hollandsworth, J. G., Glazeski, R. C., & Dressel, M. R. Use of social skills training in the treatment of extreme anxiety and deficient verbal skills in the job interview setting. *Journal of Applied Behavior Analysis*, 1978, *11*, 259–269.

Holmes, M. & Kagel, A. SCAN Volunteer Service, Inc., Little Rock, Arkansas. In *Child abuse and neglect programs: practice and theory*. Washington, DC: DHEW, National Institute of Mental Health, 1977.

Holmes, S. A., Barnhart, C., Cantoni, L., & Reymer, E. Working with the parent in child abuse cases. *Social Casework*, 1975, *56*, 3–12.

Holter, J. C., & Friedman, S. B. Child abuse: Early case finding in the emergency department. *Pediatrics*, 1968, *42*, 128–138. (a)

Holter, J. C., & Friedman, S. B. Principles of management in child abuse cases. *American Journal of Orthopsychiatry*, 1968, *38*, 127–136. (b)

Jacobsen, E. *Progressive relaxation*. Chicago: University of Chicago Press, 1938.

Jacobsen, E. *Modern treatment of tense patients*. Springfield, IL: Charles C. Thomas, 1970.

Johnson, B. & Morse, H. Injured children and their parents. *Children*, 1968, *15*, 147–152.

Jones, R. J. & Azrin, N. H. An experimental application of a social reinforcement approach to the problem of job finding. *Journal of Applied Behavior Analysis*, 1973, *6*, 345–353.

Kelly, J. A. *Social skills training: A practical guide for intervention*. New York: Springer, 1982. (a)

Kelly, J. A. Final report on the Mississippi WIN-CETA Job Search Project. WIN Program, Mississippi Department of Public Welfare, 1982. (b)

Kelly, J. A. *Solving your child's behavior problems: An everyday guide for parents*. Boston: Little, Brown, 1983.

Kelly, J. A., Wildman, B. G., & Berler, E. S. Small group behavioral training to improve the job interview skills repertoire of mildly retarded adolescents. *Journal of Applied Behavior Analysis*, 1980, *13*, 461–471.

Kelly, J. F. Extinction-induced aggression in humans. Unpublished master's thesis, Southern Illinois University, 1969.

Kempe, C. H. A practical approach to protection of the abused child and rehabilitation of the abusing parent. *Pediatrics*, 1973, *51*, 804–812.

Kempe, C. H. & Helfer, R. E. *Helping the battered child and his family*. Philadelphia: J. B. Lippincott, 1972.

Kempe, C. H., Silverman, F. N., Steele, B. F., Droegenmueller, W., & Silver, H. K. The battered child syndrome. *Journal of the American Medical Association*, 1962, *181*, 17–24.

Kempe, R. & Kempe, C. H. Assessing family pathology. In R. E. Helfer & C. H. Kempe (Eds.), *Child abuse and neglect.* Cambridge, MA: Ballinger, 1976.

Kempe, R. S. & Kempe, C. H. *Child abuse.* Cambridge, MA: Harvard University Press, 1978.

Klein, D. C. & Goldston, S. E. Proceedings of the Pilot Conference on Primary Prevention, April, 1976. Rockville, MD: National Institute of Mental Health, Department of Health, Education, and Welfare, 1977.

Knight, M., Disbrow, M., & Doer, H. Prediction of child abuse and neglect: Measures to identify parents' potential. In M. L. Lauderdale, R. N. Anderson, & S. E. Cramer (Eds.), *Child abuse and neglect: Issues on innovation and implementation. Proceedings of the Second Annual National Conference on Child Abuse and Neglect* (Vol. II). Washington, DC: U.S. Government Printing Office, 1978 (DHEW Publication No. (OHDS)78-30148).

Korbin, J. Anthropological contributions to the study of child abuse. *Child Abuse and Neglect,* 1977, *1,* 7–24.

Lavigueur, H., Peterson, R. F., Sheese, J. G., & Peterson, L. W. Behavioral treatment in the home: Effects on an untreated sibling and long-term follow-up. *Behavior Therapy,* 1973, *4,* 431–441.

Lazarus, A. *Behavior therapy and beyond.* New York: McGraw-Hill, 1971.

Lazarus, R. *Psychological stress and the coping process.* New York: McGraw-Hill, 1966.

Leitenberg, H., Burchard, J. D., Burchard, S. N., Fuller, E. M., & Lysaght, T. V. Using positive reinforcement to suppress behavior: Some experimental comparisons with sibling conflict. *Behavior Therapy,* 1977, *8,* 168–182.

Light, R. J. Abused and neglected children in America: A study of alternative policies. *Harvard Educational Review,* 1973, *43,* 556–598.

Linehan, M. M., Goldfried, M., & Goldfried. A. Assertion training: Skill training or cognitive restructuring. *Behavior Therapy,* 1979, *1,* 372–388.

Lovaas, O. I. Effect of exposure to symbolic aggression on aggressive behavior. *Child Development,* 1961, *32,* 37–44.

Mahoney, M. J. *Cognition and behavior modification.* Cambridge, MA: Ballinger, 1974.

Mahoney, M. J. Reflections on the cognitive-learning trend in psychotherapy. *American Psychologist,* 1977, *32,* 5–13.

Mahoney, M. J. & Arnkoff, D. Cognitive and self-control therapies. In S. C. Garfield & A. E. Bergin (Eds.), *Handbook of psychotherapy and behavior change.* (2nd ed.). New York: Wiley, 1977.

Martin, H. P., Beezley, P., Conway, E. F., & Kempe, C. H. The development of abused children. *Advances in Pediatrics,* 1974, *21,* 25–73.

Mastria, E. O., Mastria, M. A., & Harkins, J. C. Treatment of child abuse by behavioral intervention: A case report. *Child Welfare,* 1979, *58,* 253–261.

McRae, K. N., Ferguson, C. A., & Lederman, R. S. The battered child syndrome. *Canadian Medical Association Journal,* 1973, *108,* 859–866.

Meehan, E. J. & Ganson, H. Final report: Evaluation of the WIN Total Registrant Involvement Project. Report prepared for U.S. Department of Labor, Employment and Training Administration, 1982.

Meichenbaum, D. *Cognitive behavior modification.* Morristown, NJ: General Learning Press, 1974.

Meichenbaum, D. Self-instructional methods. In F. H. Kanfer & A. P. Goldstein (Eds.), *Helping people change.* New York: Pergamon Press, 1975.

Meichenbaum, D. *Cognitive behavior modification.* New York: Plenum Press, 1977.

Meichenbaum, D. & Cameron, R. Stress inoculation: A skills training approach to anxiety management. Unpublished manuscript, University of Waterloo, Ontario, Canada, 1973.

Merrill, E. J. Physical abuse of children. In *Protecting the battered child.* Denver: American Humane Association, Children's Division, 1962.

Miller, D. S. Fractures among children: Parental assault as causative agent. *Minnesota Medicine,* 1959, *42,* 1209–1213.

Miller, K. L. *Principles of everyday behavior analysis* (2nd ed.). Monterey, CA: Brooks/Cole Publishing Co., 1980.

Milow, I. & Lourie, R. The child's role in the battered child syndrome. *Society for Pediatric Research,* 1964, *65,* 1079–1081.

Minkin, N., Braukman, C. J., Minkin, B. L., Timbers, G. D., Timbers, B. J., Fixsen, D. J., Phillips, E. L., & Wolf, M. M. The social validation and training of conversational skills. *Journal of Applied Behavior Analysis,* 1976, *9,* 127–139.

Mischel, W. *Personality and assessment.* New York: Wiley, 1968.

Moore, J. G. Yo-yo children: Victims of matrimonial violence. *Child Welfare,* 1975, *54,* 557–566.

Morse, C. W., Sahler, O. J. Z., & Friedman, S. B. A three-year followup study of abused and neglected children. *American Journal of Diseases of Children,* 1970, *120,* 439–446.

Newcomer, P. L. *Understanding and teaching emotionally disturbed children.* Boston: Allyn and Bacon, 1980.

Novaco, R. W. *Anger control: The development and evaluation of an experimental treatment.* Lexington, MA: D. C. Heath, Lexington Books, 1975.

Novaco, R. W. Treatment of chronic anger through cognitive and relaxation controls. *Journal of Consulting and Clinical Psychology,* 1976, *44,* 681.

Novaco, R. W. Stress inoculation: A cognitive therapy for anger and its application to a case of depression. *Journal of Consulting and Clinical Psychology,* 1977, *45,* 600–608.

Novaco, R. W. Anger and coping with stress. In J. P. Foreyt & D. P. Rathjen (Eds.), *Cognitive behavior therapy: Research and application.* New York: Plenum Press, 1978.

Nurse, S. M. Familial patterns of parents who abuse their children. *Smith College Studies on Social Work,* 1964, *32,* 11–25.

O'Dell, S. L., Tarler-Benlolo, L., & Flynn, J. M. An instrument to measure knowledge of behavioral principles as applied to children. *Journal of Behavior Therapy and Experimental Psychiatry,* 1979, *10,* 29–34.

Ory, M. G. & Earp, J. L. Child maltreatment: An analysis of familial and institutional predictors. *Journal of Family Issues,* 1980, *1,* 339–356.

Parke, R. & Collmer, M. Child abuse: An interdisciplinary analysis. In M. Hetherington (Ed.), *Review of child development research.* Chicago: University of Chicago Press, 1975.

Patterson, G. R. *Families: Application of social learning to family life.* Champaign, IL: Research Press, 1974.

Patterson, G. R. The aggressive child: Victim and architect of a coercive system. In L. A. Hamerlynck, L. C. Handy, & E. J. Mash (Eds.), *Behavior modification and families. I. Theory and research.* New York: Brunner/Mazel, 1976.

Patterson, G. R. A performance theory for coercive family interaction. In R. Cairns

(Ed.), *Social interactions: Methods, analysis, and illustrations.* Society Research Child Development Monographs, 1977.

Patterson, G. R., Ray, R., Shaw, D., & Cobb, T. *A manual for coding family interactions.* New York: Microfiche Publications, 1969.

Paulson, M. J., Afifi, A., Thomason, M. L., & Chaleef, A. The MMPI: A descriptive measure of psychopathology in abusive parents. *Journal of Clinical Psychology*, 1974, *30*, 387–390.

Pelton, L. H. Child abuse and neglect: The myth of classlessness. *American Journal of Orthopsychiatry*, 1978, *48*, 608–617.

Pelton, L. H. Interpreting family violence data. *American Journal of Orthopsychiatry*, 1979, *49*, 194.

Platt, J. J., Spivak, G., Altman, N., & Altman, D. Adolescent problem-solving thinking. *Journal of Consulting and Clinical Psychology*, 1974, *42*, 787–793.

Polansky, N. A., Hally, C., & Polansky, N. F. *Profile of neglect.* Washington, DC: Social and Rehabilitation Service, 1975.

Rapoport, L. The concept of prevention in social work. *Social Work*, 1961, *6*, 3–12.

Resick, P. A. & Sweet, J. J. Child maltreatment intervention: Directions and issues. *Journal of Social Issues*, 1979, *35*, 140–160.

Rettig, E. B. *ABCs for parents.* Van Nuys, CA: Associates for Behavior Change, 1973.

Reynolds, G. S. *A primer of operant conditioning* (revised ed.). Glenview, IL: Scott, Foresman, and Co., 1975.

Rimm, D. C. & Masters, J. C. *Behavior therapy: Techniques and empirical findings* (2nd ed.). New York: Academic Press, 1979.

Roberts, M. W., McMahon, R. J., Forehand, R., & Humphreys, L. The effects of parental instruction-giving on child compliance. *Behavior Therapy*, 1978, *9*, 793–798.

Rotter, J. B. *Social learning and clinical psychology.* New York: Prentice-Hall, 1954.

Rule, B. G. & Nesdale, A. R. Emotional arousal and aggressive behavior. *Psychological Bulletin*, 1976, *83*, 851–863.

Sandler, J., Van Dercar, C., & Milhoan, M. Training child abusers in the use of positive reinforcement practices. *Behavior Research and Therapy*, 1978, *16*, 169–175.

Schechter, M. D. & Roberge, L. Sexual exploitation. In R. E. Helfer & C. F. Kempe (Eds.), *Child abuse and neglect.* Cambridge, MA: Ballinger, 1976.

Scott, P. D. Fatal battered baby cases. *Medicine, Science and the Law*, 1973, *13*, 197–206.

Scott, P. M., Burton, R. V., and Yarrow, M. R. Social reinforcement under natural conditions. *Child Development*, 1967, *38*, 53–63.

Scott, W. O. N., Baer, G., Christoff, K., and Kelly, J. A. Skills training for a child abusive parent: A controlled case study. Unpublished manuscript, University of Mississippi Medical Center, 1982.

Shorkey, C. T. Psychological characteristics of child abusers: Speculation and the need for research. *Child Abuse and Neglect*, 1978, *2*, 69–76.

Silver, L. B. Child abuse syndrome: A review. *Medical Times*, 1968, *96*, 803–820.

Silver, L. B., Dublin, C. C., & Lourie, R. S. Does violence breed violence? Contributions from a study of the child abuse syndrome. *American Journal of Psychiatry*, 1969, *126*, 152–155.

Smith, S. M. *The battered child syndrome.* London: Butterworths, 1975.

Smith, S. M. & Hanson, R. 134 battered children: A medical and psychological study. *British Medical Journal*, 1974, *3*, 666–670.

Smith, S. M. & Hanson, R. Interpersonal relationships and child-rearing practices in six parents of battered children. *British Journal of Psychiatry,* 1975, *125,* 513–525.

Smith, S. M., Hanson, R., & Noble, S. Parents of battered babies: A controlled study. *British Medical Journal,* 1973, *4,* 388–391.

Smith, S. M., Hanson, R., & Noble, S. Social aspects of the battered baby syndrome. *British Journal of Psychiatry,* 1974, *125,* 568–582.

Spinetta, J. J. & Rigler, D. The child-abusing parent: A psychological review. *Psychological Bulletin,* 1972, *77,* 296–304.

Spinetta, J. J. Parental personality factors in child abuse. *Journal of Consulting and Clinical Psychology,* 1978, *46,* 1409–1414.

Spivak, G., Platt, J. J., & Shure, M. B. *The problem-solving approach to adjustment—research and intervention.* San Francisco: Jossey-Bass, 1976.

Statistical Report on Child Abuse and Neglect in Hawaii. State of Hawaii, Department of Social Services and Housing, 1975.

Steele, B. F. Experience with an interdisciplinary concept. In R. E. Helfer & C. H. Kempe (Eds.), *Child abuse and neglect: The family and the community.* Cambridge, MA: Ballinger, 1976.

Steele, B. F. & Pollock, C. B. A psychiatric study of parents who abuse infants and small children. In R. E. Helfer & C. H. Kempe (Eds.), *The battered child.* Chicago: University of Chicago Press, 1968.

Stein, T., Gambrill, E., & Wiltse, K. Foster care: The rise of contracts. *Public Welfare,* 1974, 20–25.

Strober, M. & Bellack, A. S. Multiple component behavioral treatment for a child with behavior problems. *Journal of Behavior Therapy and Experimental Psychiatry,* 1975, *6,* 250–252.

Stumphauzer, J. S. A low-cost "bug-in-the ear" sound system for modification of therapist, parent, and patient behavior. *Behavior Therapy,* 1971, *2,* 249–250.

Sulzer-Azaroff, B. & Mayer, G. R. *Applying behavior analysis procedures with children and youth.* New York: Holt, Rinehart & Winston, 1977.

Sundel, M. & Homan, C. C. Prevention in child welfare: A framework for management and practice. *Child Welfare,* 1979, *58,* 510–521.

Swanson, D. Adult sexual abuse of children. *Diseases of the Nervous System,* 1968, *29,* 677–688.

Wahler, R. G. Oppositional children: A guest for parental reinforcement control. *Journal of Applied Behavior Analysis,* 1969, *2,* 159–170.

Wahler, R. G. The insular mother: Her problem in parent–child treatment. *Journal of Applied Behavior Analysis,* 1980, *13,* 207–219.

Wahler, R. G., Leske, G., & Rogers, E. S. The insular family: A deviance support system for oppositional children. In L. A. Hamerlynck (Ed.), *Behavioral systems for the developmentally disabled: I. School and family environments.* New York: Brunner/Mazel, 1979.

Wasserman, S. The abused parent of the abused child. *Children,* 1967, *14,* 175–179.

Watkins, H. D. & Bradbard, M. R. Child maltreatment: An overview with suggestions for intervention and research. *Family Relations,* 1982, *31,* 323–333.

Weiss, R. C., Hops, H., & Patterson, G. R. A framework for conceptualizing marital conflict, a technology for altering it, some data for evaluating it. In L. A.

Hamerlynck, L. C. Handy, & E. J. Marsh (Eds.), *Behavior change: Methodology, concepts and practice*. Champaign, IL: Research Press, 1973.

Weston, J. T. The pathology of child abuse. In R. Helfer, & C. H. Kempe (Eds.), *The battered child*. Chicago: University of Chicago Press, 1968.

Wodarski, J. S. Comprehensive treatment of parents who abuse their children. *Adolescence*, 1981, *16*, 959–972.

Wolf, M. M., Risley, T. R., Johnson, M., Harris, F., & Allen, E. Application of operant conditioning principles to the behavior problems of an autistic child: A followup extension. *Behavior Research and Therapy*, 1967, *5*, 103–112.

Wolf, M. M., Risley, T. R., & Mees, H. L. Application of operant conditioning procedures to the behavior problems of an autistic child. *Behavior Research and Therapy*, 1964, *1*, 303–312.

Wolfe, D. A., Fairbank, J. A., Kelly, J. A., & Bradlyn, A. S. Child abusive parents: Physiological responses to stressful and nonstressful behavior in children. *Behavioral Assessment*, in press.

Wolfe, D. A., Kaufman, K., Aragona, J., & Sandler, J. *The child management program for abusive parents*. Winter Park, FL: Anna Publishing, 1981.

Wolfe, D. A., Kelly, J. A., & Drabman, R. S. "Beat the buzzer": A method for training an abusive mother to decrease recurrent child conflicts. *Journal of Clinical Child Psychology*, 1981, *10*, 114–116. (b)

Wolfe, D. A. & Sandler, J. Training abusive parents in effective child management. *Behavior Modification*, 1981, *5*, 320–335.

Wolfe, D. A., Sandler, J., & Kaufman, K. A competency-based parent training program for child abusers. *Journal of Consulting and Clinical Psychology*, 1981, *49*, 633–640. (c)

Wolfe, D. A., St. Lawrence, J. S., Graves, K., Brehony, K., Bradlyn, A. S., & Kelly, J. A. Intensive behavioral parent training for a child abusive mother. *Behavior Therapy*, 1982, *13*, 438–451.

Wolpe, J. *Psychotherapy by reciprocal inhibition*. Stanford: Stanford University Press, 1958.

Wolpe, J. *Practice of behavior therapy* (2nd ed.). New York: Pergamon Press, 1973.

Woolley, P. V. & Evans, W. A. Significance of skeletal lesions in infants resembling those of traumatic origin. *Journal of the American Medical Association*, 1955, *158*, 539–543.

Wright, L. The "sick but slick" syndrome as a personality component of parents of battered children. *Journal of Clinical Psychology*, 1976, *32*, 41–45.

Yerkes, R. M. & Dodson, J. D. The relation of strength of stimulus to rapidity of habit-formation. *Journal of Comparative Neurology and Psychology*, 1908, *18*, 459–482.

Young, L. *Wednesday's children: A study of child neglect and abuse*. New York: McGraw-Hill, 1964.

Zalba, S. R. The abused child: A typology for classification and treatment. *Social Work*, 1967, *12*, 70–79.

Zeilberger, J., Sampen, S. E., & Sloane, H. N. Modification of a child's problem behavior in the home with the mother as therapist. *Journal of Applied Behavior Analysis*, 1968, *1*, 47–53.

Author Index

Subject Index

Breinigsville, PA USA
29 December 2010

252022BV00006B/27/A

9 780306 414176